HAROLD PINTER
PLAYS FOUR

Betrayal, Monologue, One for the Road,
Mountain Language, Family Voices, A Kind of Alaska,
Victoria Station, Precisely, The New World Order,
Party Time, Moonlight, Ashes to Ashes, Celebration

Harold Pinter was born in London in 1930. He is married to Antonia Fraser. In 1995 he won the David Cohen British Literature Prize, awarded for a lifetime's achievement in literature. In 1996 he was given the Laurence Olivier Award for a lifetime's achievement in theatre. In 2002 he was made a Companion of Honour for services to literature. In 2005 he received the Wilfred Owen Award for Poetry, the Franz Kafka Award (Prague) and the Nobel Prize for Literature.

HAROLD PINTER

Plays Four

Betrayal

Monologue

One for the Road

Mountain Language

Family Voices

A Kind of Alaska

Victoria Station

Precisely

The New World Order

Party Time

Moonlight

Ashes to Ashes

Celebration

faber and faber

This collection first published in 1993 by Faber and Faber Limited
3 Queen Square London WC1N 3AU
Reissued as *Harold Pinter: Plays Four* in 1996
Expanded edition (including *Moonlight* and *Ashes to Ashes*)
first published in 1998
Second expanded edition (including *Celebration*) first published in 2005

Photoset by Parker Typesetting Service, Leicester
Printed in England by Mackays of Chatham PLC, Chatham, Kent

Betrayal first published by Eyre Methuen Ltd in 1978, revised in 1980
Monologue first published in limited edition only in 1973
Family Voices first published by Next Editions in 1981
One for the Road first published by Methuen London Ltd in 1984
A Kind of Alaska first published by Methuen London Ltd in 1982
Victoria Station first published by Methuen London Ltd in 1982
Mountain Language first published by Faber and Faber Ltd in 1988
Precisely first published in *The Big One* by Methuen London Ltd in 1984
The New World Order first published in *Granta* (No. 37) in Autumn 1991
Party Time first published by Faber and Faber Ltd in 1991
Moonlight first published by Faber and Faber Ltd in 1993
Ashes to Ashes first published by Faber and Faber Ltd in 1996
Celebration first published by Faber and Faber Ltd in 2000

All rights whatsoever in these plays are strictly reserved and applications to
perform them should be made in writing, before rehearsals begin, to Judy Daish
Associates, 1 St Charles Place, London W10 6EG

A CIP record for this book is available from the British Library

ISBN 978-0-571-23223-9
ISBN 0-571-23223-X

2 4 6 8 10 9 7 5 3

Contents

Introduction

Harold Pinter's speech of thanks on receiving the David Cohen British Literature Prize for 1995. The Prize is awarded every two years in recognition of a lifetime's achievement by a living British writer.

This is a great honour. Thank you very much.

I can't say that there was a very strong literary tradition in my family. My mother enjoyed reading the novels of A. J. Cronin and Arnold Bennett and my father (who left the house at 7.00 am and returned at 7.00 pm, working as a jobbing tailor) liked Westerns but there were very few books about the house. This was of course also due to the fact that we depended entirely upon libraries. Nobody could afford to buy books.

However, when I first had a poem published in a magazine called *Poetry London* my parents were quite pleased. I published the poem with my name spelt PINTA, as one of my aunts was convinced that we came from a distinguished Portuguese family, the Da Pintas. This has never been confirmed, nor do I know whether such a family ever existed. The whole thing seemed to be in quite violent conflict with my understanding that all four of my grandparents came from Odessa, or at least Hungary or perhaps even Poland.

There was tentative speculation that PINTA became PINTER in the course of flight from the Spanish Inquisition but whether they had a Spanish Inquisition in Portugal no one quite seemed to know, at least in Hackney, where we lived. Anyway I found the PINTA spelling quite attractive, although I didn't go as far as the 'DA'. And I dropped the whole idea shortly afterwards.

There was only one member of my family who appeared to be at all well-off, my great-uncle, Uncle Coleman, who was 'in business'. He always wore felt carpet-slippers and a skull cap at home and was a very courteous man. My father proposed that I show Uncle Coleman my poem in *Poetry London* when we next went to tea. I agreed, with some misgivings. My poem was called 'New Year in the Midlands' and was to do with a young actor's vagabond life in rep. It was heavily influenced by Dylan Thomas. It contained the following lines:

'This is the shine, the powder and blood and here am I,
Straddled, exile always in one Whitbread Ale town,
Or such.

My father and I sat in the room in silence, while Uncle Coleman read this poem. When he reached those lines he stopped, looked over the magazine at us and said: 'Whitbread shares are doing very well at the moment. Take my tip.'

That was in 1950, when I was 20.

My early reading was rather shapeless and disjointed, mainly, I believe, to do with the dislocation of a childhood in wartime. I was evacuated twice (once to Cornwall, where I more or less saw the sea for the first time) went to a number of schools and kept returning to London to more bombs, flying bombs and rockets. It wasn't a very conducive atmosphere for reading. But I finally settled in Hackney Downs Grammar School in late 1944 and made up for lost time. Hackney also had a great Public Library and there I discovered Joyce,

Lawrence, Dostoevsky, Hemingway, Virginia Woolf, Rimbaud, Yeats etc.

Some years later, in I think 1951, having read an extract from Beckett's *Watt* in a magazine called *Irish Writing*, I looked for books by Beckett in library after library – with no success. Eventually I unearthed one – his first novel *Murphy*. It had been hanging about Bermondsey Public Reserve Library since 1938. I concluded that interest in Beckett was low and decided to keep it - on an extended loan, as it were. I still have it.

In 1944 I met Joseph Brearley, who came to the school to teach English. Joe Brearley was a tall Yorkshireman who suffered from malaria, had been torpedoed at sea in the war and possessed a passionate enthusiasm for English poetry and dramatic literature. There had been no drama in the school when he arrived in 1945 but before we knew where we were he announced that he would do a production of *Macbeth* and pointing at me in class said: 'And you, Pinter, will play Macbeth.' 'Me, sir?' I said. 'Yes. You.' he said. I was 15 and I did play Macbeth, in modern dress, wearing the uniform of a major-general. I was so pleased with this uniform that I wore it on the 38 bus to go home to tea after the dress rehearsal. Old ladies smiled at me. The bus conductor looked at me and said: 'Well, I don't know what to charge you.' My parents gave me the *Collected Plays of Shakespeare* to mark the occasion. I also managed to save up to buy a copy of *Ulysses* which I placed on the bookshelf in the living room. My father told me to take it off the shelf. He said he wouldn't have a book like that in the room where my mother served dinner.

Joe Brearley and I became close friends. We embarked

on a series of long walks, which continued for years, starting from Hackney Downs, up to Springfield Park, along the River Lea, back up Lea Bridge Road, past Clapton Pond, through Mare Street to Bethnal Green. Shakespeare dominated our lives at that time (I mean the lives of my friends and me) but the revelation which Joe Brearley brought with him was John Webster. On our walks, we would declare into the wind, at the passing trolley-buses or indeed to the passers-by, nuggets of Webster, such as:

> What would it pleasure me to have my throat cut
> With diamonds? or to be smothered
> With Cassia? or to be shot to death with pearls?
> I know death hath ten thousand several doors
> For men to take their exits: and tis found
> They go on such strange geometric hinges
> You may open them both ways: anyway, for
>   heaven's sake,
> So I were out of your whispering.
> (*The Duchess of Malfi*)

or:

> O I smell soot,
> Most stinking soot, the chimney's a-fire,
> My liver's purboiled like scotch holly-bread,
> There's a plumber laying pipes in my guts.
> (*The White Devil*)

or:

> My soul, like to a ship in a black storm,
> Is driven I know not whither.
> (*The White Devil*)

x

or:

> I have caught
> An everlasting cold. I have lost my voice
> Most irrecoverably.
> (*The White Devil*)

or:

> Cover her face; mine eyes dazzle; she died young.
> (*The Duchess of Malfi*)

That language made me dizzy.

Joe Brearley fired my imagination. I can never forget him.

I started writing plays in 1957 and in 1958 *The Birthday Party* opened at the Lyric, Hammersmith, was massacred by the critics (with the exception of Harold Hobson) and was taken off after eight performances. I decided to pop in to the Thursday matinee. I was a few minutes late and the curtain had gone up. I ran up the stairs to the dress circle. An usherette stopped me. 'Where are you going?' she said. 'To the dress circle,' I said, 'I'm the author.' Her eyes, as I recall, misted over. 'Oh are you?' she said, 'Oh you poor chap. Listen, the dress circle's closed, but why don't you go in, go in and sit down, darling, if you like, go on.' I went into the empty dress circle and looked down into the stalls. Six people were watching the performance which, I must say, didn't seem to be generating very much electricity. I still have the box-office returns for the week. The Thursday matinee brought in two pounds six shillings.

In a career attended by a great deal of dramatic

criticism one of the most interesting – and indeed acute – critical questions I've ever heard was when I was introduced to a young woman and her six-year-old son. The woman looked down at her son and said: 'This man is a very good writer.' The little boy looked at me and then at his mother and said: 'Can he do a "W"?'

I'm well aware that I have been described in some quarters as being 'enigmatic, taciturn, terse, prickly, explosive and forbidding'. Well, I do have my moods like anyone else, I won't deny it. But my writing life, which has gone on for roughly 45 years and isn't over yet, has been informed by a quite different set of characteristics which have nothing whatsoever to do with those descriptions. Quite simply, my writing life has been one of relish, challenge, excitement. Those words are almost, perhaps, truisms. But in fact they are true. Whether it be a poem, a play or a screenplay – if the relish, challenge and excitement in the language and through that language to character isn't there then nothing's there and nothing can exist.

So while I'm sure I am 'enigmatic, taciturn, terse, prickly, explosive and forbidding' I've also enjoyed my writing life – and indeed my life – to the hilt and I am deeply gratified to have been awarded this prize.

BETRAYAL

Betrayal was first presented by the National Theatre, London, on 15 November 1978 with the following cast:

EMMA   Penelope Wilton
JERRY   Michael Gambon
ROBERT   Daniel Massey

Directed by Peter Hall
Designed by John Bury

In 1977 Emma is 38, Jerry and Robert are 40.

Betrayal can be performed without an interval, or with an interval after Scene Four.

H.P.

1977

SCENE ONE
Pub. 1977. Spring.

Noon.

EMMA is sitting at a corner table. JERRY approaches with drinks, a pint of bitter for him, a glass of wine for her.

He sits. They smile, toast each other silently, drink.

He sits back and looks at her.

JERRY

Well . . .

EMMA

How are you?

JERRY

All right.

EMMA

You look well.

JERRY

Well, I'm not all that well, really.

EMMA

Why? What's the matter?

3

JERRY

Hangover.

He raises his glass.

Cheers.

He drinks.

How are you?

EMMA

I'm fine.

She looks round the bar, back at him.

Just like old times.

JERRY

Mmm. It's been a long time.

EMMA

Yes.

Pause.

I thought of you the other day.

JERRY

Good God. Why?

She laughs.

4

JERRY

Why?

EMMA

Well, it's nice, sometimes, to think back. Isn't it?

JERRY

Absolutely.

Pause.

How's everything?

EMMA

Oh, not too bad.

Pause.

Do you know how long it is since we met?

JERRY

Well I came to that private view, when was it – ?

EMMA

No, I don't mean that.

JERRY

Oh you mean alone?

EMMA

Yes.

JERRY

Uuh . . .

EMMA

Two years.

JERRY

Yes, I thought it must be. Mmnn.

Pause.

EMMA

Long time.

JERRY

Yes. It is.

Pause.

How's it going? The Gallery?

EMMA

How do you think it's going?

JERRY

Well. Very well, I would say.

EMMA

I'm glad you think so. Well, it is actually. I enjoy it.

JERRY

Funny lot, painters, aren't they?

EMMA

They're not at all funny.

JERRY

Aren't they? What a pity.

Pause.

How's Robert?

EMMA

When did you last see him?

JERRY

I haven't seen him for months. Don't know why.
Why?

EMMA

Why what?

JERRY

Why did you ask when I last saw him?

EMMA

I just wondered. How's Sam?

JERRY

You mean Judith.

EMMA

Do I?

7

JERRY

You remember the form. I ask about your husband, you ask about my wife.

EMMA

Yes, of course. How is your wife?

JERRY

All right.

Pause.

EMMA

Sam must be . . . tall.

JERRY

He is tall. Quite tall. Does a lot of running. He's a long distance runner. He wants to be a zoologist.

EMMA

No, really? Good. And Sarah?

JERRY

She's ten.

EMMA

God. I suppose she must be.

JERRY

Yes, she must be.

Pause.

8

Ned's five, isn't he?

EMMA

You remember.

JERRY

Well, I would remember that.

Pause.

EMMA

Yes.

Pause.

You're all right, though?

JERRY

Oh . . . yes, sure.

Pause.

EMMA

Ever think of me?

JERRY

I don't need to think of you.

EMMA

Oh?

JERRY

I don't need to *think* of you.

Pause.

Anyway I'm all right. How are you?

EMMA

Fine, really. All right.

JERRY

You're looking very pretty.

EMMA

Really? Thank you. I'm glad to see you.

JERRY

So am I. I mean to see you.

EMMA

You think of me sometimes?

JERRY

I think of you sometimes.

Pause.

I saw Charlotte the other day.

EMMA

No? Where? She didn't mention it.

JERRY

She didn't see me. In the street.

EMMA

But you haven't seen her for years.

JERRY

I recognised her.

EMMA

How could you? How could you know?

JERRY

I did.

EMMA

What did she look like?

JERRY

You.

EMMA

No, what did you think of her, really?

JERRY

I thought she was lovely.

EMMA

Yes. She's very . . . She's smashing. She's thirteen.

Pause.

Do you remember that time . . . oh God it was . . .
when you picked her up and threw her up and caught
her?

JERRY

She was very light.

EMMA

She remembers that, you know.

JERRY

Really?

EMMA

Mmnn. Being thrown up.

JERRY

What a memory.

Pause.

She doesn't know . . . about us, does she?

EMMA

Of course not. She just remembers you, as an old friend.

JERRY

That's right.

Pause.

Yes, everyone was there that day, standing around, your husband, my wife, all the kids, I remember.

EMMA

What day?

JERRY

When I threw her up. It was in your kitchen.

EMMA

It was in your kitchen.

Silence.

JERRY

Darling.

EMMA

Don't say that.

Pause.

It all . . .

JERRY

Seems such a long time ago.

EMMA

Does it?

JERRY

Same again?

He takes the glasses, goes to the bar. She sits still. He returns, with the drinks, sits.

EMMA

I thought of you the other day.

Pause.

I was driving through Kilburn. Suddenly I saw where I
was. I just stopped, and then I turned down Kinsale
Drive and drove into Wessex Grove. I drove past the
house and then stopped about fifty yards further on,
like we used to do, do you remember?

JERRY

Yes.

EMMA

People were coming out of the house. They walked up
the road.

JERRY

What sort of people?

EMMA

Oh . . . young people. Then I got out of the car and
went up the steps. I looked at the bells, you know, the
names on the bells. I looked for our name.

Pause.

JERRY

Green.

Pause.

Couldn't see it, eh?

EMMA

No.

JERRY

That's because we're not there any more. We haven't been there for years.

EMMA

No we haven't.

Pause.

JERRY

I hear you're seeing a bit of Casey.

EMMA

What?

JERRY

Casey. I just heard you were . . . seeing a bit of him.

EMMA

Where did you hear that?

JERRY

Oh . . . people . . . talking.

EMMA

Christ.

JERRY

The funny thing was that the only thing I really felt was irritation, I mean irritation that nobody gossiped about us like that, in the old days. I nearly said, now look, she may be having the occasional drink with Casey, who cares, but she and I had an affair for seven years and none of you bastards had the faintest idea it was happening.

Pause.

EMMA

I wonder. I wonder if everyone knew, all the time.

JERRY

Don't be silly. We were brilliant. Nobody knew. Who ever went to Kilburn in those days? Just you and me.

Pause.

Anyway, what's all this about you and Casey?

EMMA

What do you mean?

JERRY

What's going on?

EMMA

We have the occasional drink.

JERRY

I thought you didn't admire his work.

EMMA

I've changed. Or his work has changed. Are you jealous?

JERRY

Of what?

Pause.

I couldn't be jealous of Casey. I'm his agent. I advised him about his divorce. I read all his first drafts. I persuaded your husband to publish his first novel. I escort him to Oxford to speak at the Union. He's my . . . he's my boy. I discovered him when he was a poet, and that's a bloody long time ago now.

Pause.

He's even taken me down to Southampton to meet his Mum and Dad. I couldn't be jealous of Casey. Anyway it's not as if we're having an affair now, is it? We haven't seen each other for years. Really, I'm very happy if you're happy.

Pause.

What about Robert?

Pause.

EMMA

Well . . . I think we're going to separate.

JERRY

Oh?

EMMA

We had a long talk . . . last night.

JERRY

Last night?

EMMA

You know what I found out . . . last night? He's
betrayed me for years. He's had . . . other women for
years.

JERRY

No? Good Lord.

Pause.

But we betrayed him for years.

EMMA

And he betrayed me for years.

JERRY

Well I never knew that.

EMMA

Nor did I.

Pause.

JERRY

Does Casey know about this?

EMMA

I wish you wouldn't keep calling him Casey. His name
is Roger.

JERRY

Yes. Roger.

EMMA

I phoned *you*. I don't know why.

JERRY

What a funny thing. We were such close friends, weren't
we? Robert and me, even though I haven't seem him for
a few months, but through all those years, all the
drinks, all the lunches . . . we had together, I never even
gleaned . . . I never suspected . . . that there was anyone
else . . . in his life but you. Never. For example, when
you're with a fellow in a pub, or a restaurant, for
example, from time to time he pops out for a piss, you
see, who doesn't, but what I mean is, if he's making a
crafty telephone call, you can sort of sense it, you see,
you can sense the pip pip pips. Well, I never did that
with Robert. He never made any pip pip telephone calls
in any pub I was ever with him in. The funny thing is
that it was me who made the pip pip calls – to you,
when I left him boozing at the bar. That's the funny
thing.

Pause.

When did he tell you all this?

19

EMMA

Last night. I think we were up all night.

Pause.

JERRY

You talked all night?

EMMA

Yes. Oh yes.

Pause.

JERRY

I didn't come into it, did I?

EMMA

What?

JERRY

I just –

EMMA

I just phoned you this morning, you know, that's all, because I . . . because we're old friends . . . I've been up all night . . . the whole thing's finished . . . I suddenly felt I wanted to see you.

JERRY

Well, look, I'm happy to see you. I am. I'm sorry . . . about . . .

EMMA

Do you remember? I mean, you do remember?

JERRY

I remember.

Pause.

EMMA

You couldn't really afford Wessex Grove when we took it, could you?

JERRY

Oh, love finds a way.

EMMA

I bought the curtains.

JERRY

You found a way.

EMMA

Listen, I didn't want to see you for nostalgia, I mean what's the point? I just wanted to see how you were. Truly. How are you?

JERRY

Oh what does it matter?

Pause.

You didn't tell Robert about me last night, did you?

EMMA

I had to.

Pause.

He told me everything. I told him everything. We were up . . . all night. At one point Ned came down. I had to take him up to bed, had to put him back to bed. Then I went down again. I think it was the voices woke him up. You know . . .

JERRY

You told him everything?

EMMA

I had to.

JERRY

You told him everything . . . about us?

EMMA

I had to.

Pause.

JERRY

But he's my oldest friend. I mean, I picked his own daughter up in my own arms and threw her up and caught her, in my kitchen. He watched me do it.

EMMA

It doesn't matter. It's all gone.

JERRY

Is it? What has?

EMMA

It's all all over.

She drinks.

1977 Later

SCENE TWO
Jerry's House. Study. 1977. Spring.

JERRY *sitting.* ROBERT *standing, with glass.*

JERRY
It's good of you to come.

ROBERT
Not at all.

JERRY
Yes, yes, I know it was difficult . . . I know . . . the kids . . .

ROBERT
It's all right. It sounded urgent.

JERRY
Well . . . You found someone, did you?

ROBERT
What?

JERRY
For the kids.

ROBERT
Yes, yes. Honestly. Everything's in order. Anyway, Charlotte's not a baby.

JERRY

No.

Pause.

Are you going to sit down?

ROBERT

Well, I might, yes, in a minute.

Pause.

JERRY

Judith's at the hospital . . . on night duty. The kids are
. . . here . . . upstairs.

ROBERT

Uh – huh.

JERRY

I must speak to you. It's important.

ROBERT

Speak.

JERRY

Yes.

Pause.

ROBERT

You look quite rough.

Pause.

What's the trouble?

Pause.

It's not about you and Emma, is it?

Pause.

I know all about that.

JERRY
Yes. So I've . . . been told.

ROBERT
Ah.

Pause.

Well, it's not very important, is it? Been over for years, hasn't it?

JERRY
It is important.

ROBERT
Really? Why?

JERRY *stands, walks about.*

JERRY
I thought I was going to go mad.

ROBERT

When?

JERRY

This evening. Just now. Wondering whether to phone
you. I had to phone you. It took me . . . two hours to
phone you. And then you were with the kids . . . I
thought I wasn't going to be able to see you . . . I
thought I'd go mad. I'm very grateful to you . . . for
coming.

ROBERT

Oh for God's sake! Look, what exactly do you want to
say?

Pause.

JERRY *sits.*

JERRY

I don't know why she told you. I don't know how she
could tell you. I just don't understand. Listen, I know
you've got . . . look, I saw her today . . . we had a drink
. . . I haven't seen her for . . . she told me, you know,
that you're in trouble, both of you . . . and so on. I
know that. I mean I'm sorry.

ROBERT

Don't be sorry.

JERRY

Why not?

Pause.

The fact is I can't understand . . . why she thought it necessary . . . after all these years . . . to tell you . . . so suddenly . . . last night . . .

ROBERT

Last night?

JERRY

Without consulting me. Without even warning me. After all, you and me . . .

ROBERT

She didn't tell me last night.

JERRY

What do you mean?

Pause.

I know about last night. She told me about it. You were up all night, weren't you?

ROBERT

That's correct.

JERRY

And she told you . . . last night . . . about her and me. Did she not?

ROBERT

No, she didn't. She didn't tell me about you and her last

night. She told me about you and her four years ago.

Pause.

So she didn't have to tell me again last night. Because I knew. And she knew I knew because she told me herself four years ago.

Silence.

JERRY

What?

ROBERT

I think I will sit down.

He sits.

I thought you knew.

JERRY

Knew what?

ROBERT

That I knew. That I've known for years. I thought you knew that.

JERRY

You thought I knew?

ROBERT

She said you didn't. But I didn't believe that.

Pause.

Anyway I think I thought you knew. But you say you didn't?

JERRY

She told you . . . when?

ROBERT

Well, I found out. That's what happened. I told her I'd found out and then she . . . confirmed . . . the facts.

JERRY

When?

ROBERT

Oh, a long time ago, Jerry.

Pause.

JERRY

But we've seen each other . . . a great deal . . . over the last four years. We've had lunch.

ROBERT

Never played squash though.

JERRY

I was your best friend.

ROBERT

Well, yes, sure.

JERRY *stares at him and then holds his head in his hands.*

Oh, don't get upset. There's no point.

Silence.

JERRY *sits up.*

JERRY
Why didn't she tell me?

ROBERT
Well, I'm not her, old boy.

JERRY
Why didn't you tell me?

Pause.

ROBERT
I thought you might know.

JERRY
But you didn't know for *certain*, did you? You didn't *know*!

ROBERT
No.

JERRY
Then why didn't you tell me?

Pause.

ROBERT

Tell you what?

JERRY

That you knew. You bastard.

ROBERT

Oh, don't call me a bastard, Jerry.

Pause.

JERRY

What are we going to do?

ROBERT

You and I are not going to do anything. My marriage is finished. I've just got to make proper arrangements, that's all. About the children.

Pause.

JERRY

You hadn't thought of telling Judith?

ROBERT

Telling Judith what? Oh, about you and Emma. You mean she never knew? Are you quite sure?

Pause.

No, I hadn't thought of telling Judith, actually. You

32

don't seem to understand. You don't seem to understand that I don't give a shit about any of this. It's true I've hit Emma once or twice. But that wasn't to defend a principle. I wasn't inspired to do it from any kind of moral standpoint. I just felt like giving her a good bashing. The old itch . . . you understand.

Pause.

JERRY

But you betrayed her for years, didn't you?

ROBERT

Oh yes.

JERRY

And she never knew about it. Did she?

ROBERT

Didn't she?

Pause.

JERRY

I didn't.

ROBERT

No, you didn't know very much about anything, really, did you?

Pause.

JERRY

No.

ROBERT

Yes you did.

JERRY

Yes I did. I lived with her.

ROBERT

Yes. In the afternoons.

JERRY

Sometimes very long ones. For seven years.

ROBERT

Yes, you certainly knew all there was to know about that. About the seven years of afternoons. I don't know anything about that.

Pause.

I hope she looked after you all right.

Silence.

JERRY

We used to like each other.

ROBERT

We still do.

Pause.

34

I bumped into old Casey the other day. I believe he's having an affair with my wife. We haven't played squash for years, Casey and me. We used to have a damn good game.

JERRY

He's put on weight.

ROBERT

Yes, I thought that.

JERRY

He's over the hill.

ROBERT

Is he?

JERRY

Don't you think so?

ROBERT

In what respect?

JERRY

His work. His books.

ROBERT

Oh his books. His art. Yes his art does seem to be falling away, doesn't it?

JERRY

Still sells.

ROBERT

Oh, sells very well. Sells very well indeed. Very good for us. For you and me.

JERRY

Yes.

ROBERT

Someone was telling me – who was it – must have been someone in the publicity department – the other day – that when Casey went up to York to sign his latest book, in a bookshop, you know, with Barbara Spring, you know, the populace queued for hours to get his signature on his book, while one old lady and a dog queued to get Barbara Spring's signature, on her book. I happen to think that Barbara Spring . . . is good, don't you?

JERRY

Yes.

Pause.

ROBERT

Still, we both do very well out of Casey, don't we?

JERRY

Very well.

Pause.

ROBERT

Have you read any good books lately?

JERRY

I've been reading Yeats.

ROBERT

Ah. Yeats. Yes.

Pause.

JERRY

You read Yeats on Torcello once.

ROBERT

On Torcello?

JERRY

Don't you remember? Years ago. You went over to Torcello in the dawn, alone. And read Yeats.

ROBERT

So I did. I told you that, yes.

Pause.

Yes.

Pause.

Where are you going this summer, you and the family?

JERRY

The Lake District.

1975

SCENE THREE
Flat. 1975. Winter.

JERRY *and* EMMA. *They are sitting.*

Silence.

JERRY
What do you want to do then?

Pause.

EMMA
I don't quite know what we're doing, any more, that's all.

JERRY
Mmnn.

Pause.

EMMA
I mean, this flat . . .

JERRY
Yes.

EMMA
Can you actually remember when we were last here?

JERRY

In the summer, was it?

EMMA

Well, was it?

JERRY

I know it seems –

EMMA

It was the beginning of September.

JERRY

Well, that's summer, isn't it?

EMMA

It was actually extremely cold. It was early autumn.

JERRY

It's pretty cold now.

EMMA

We were going to get another electric fire.

JERRY

Yes, I never got that.

EMMA

Not much point in getting it if we're never here.

JERRY

We're here now.

EMMA

Not really.

Silence.

JERRY

Well, things have changed. You've been so busy, your job, and everything.

EMMA

Well, I know. But I mean, I like it. I want to do it.

JERRY

No, it's great. It's marvellous for you. But you're not –

EMMA

If you're running a gallery you've got to run it, you've got to be there.

JERRY

But you're not free in the afternoons. Are you?

EMMA

No.

JERRY

So how can we meet?

EMMA

But look at the times you're out of the country. You're never here.

40

JERRY

But when I am here you're not free in the afternoons. So we can never meet.

EMMA

We can meet for lunch.

JERRY

We can meet for lunch but we can't come all the way out here for a quick lunch. I'm too old for that.

EMMA

I didn't suggest that.

Pause.

You see, in the past . . . we were inventive, we were determined, it was . . . it seemed impossible to meet . . . impossible . . . and yet we did. We met here, we took this flat and we met in this flat because we wanted to.

JERRY

It would not matter how much we wanted to if you're not free in the afternoons and I'm in America.

Silence.

Nights have always been out of the question and you know it. I have a family.

EMMA

I have a family too.

JERRY

I know that perfectly well. I might remind you that your husband is my oldest friend.

EMMA

What do you mean by that?

JERRY

I don't *mean* anything by it.

EMMA

But what are you trying to say by saying that?

JERRY

Jesus. I'm not *trying* to say anything. I've said precisely what I wanted to say.

EMMA

I see.

Pause.

The fact is that in the old days we used our imagination and we'd take a night and make an arrangement and go to an hotel.

JERRY

Yes. We did.

Pause.

But that was . . . in the main . . . before we got this flat.

EMMA

We haven't spent many nights . . . in this flat.

JERRY

No.

Pause.

Not many nights anywhere, really.

Silence.

EMMA

Can you afford . . . to keep it going, month after
month?

JERRY

Oh . . .

EMMA

It's a waste. Nobody comes here. I just can't bear to
think about it, actually. Just . . . empty. All day and
night. Day after day and night after night. I mean the
crockery and the curtains and the bedspread and
everything. And the tablecloth I brought from Venice.
(*Laughs.*) It's ridiculous.

Pause.

It's just . . . an empty home.

JERRY

It's not a home.

43

Pause.

I know . . . I know what you wanted . . . but it could
never . . . actually be a home. You have a home. I have
a home. With curtains, et cetera. And children. Two
children in two homes. There are no children here, so
it's not the same kind of home.

EMMA

It was never intended to be the same kind of home. Was
it?

Pause.

You didn't ever see it as a home, in any sense, did you?

JERRY

No, I saw it as a flat . . . you know.

EMMA

For fucking.

JERRY

No, for loving.

EMMA

Well, there's not much of that left, is there?

Silence.

JERRY

I don't think we don't love each other.

44

Pause.

EMMA

Ah well.

Pause.

What will you do about all the . . . furniture?

JERRY

What?

EMMA

The contents.

Silence.

JERRY

You know we can do something very simple, if we want to do it.

EMMA

You mean sell it to Mrs Banks for a small sum and . . . and she can let it as a furnished flat?

JERRY

That's right. Wasn't the bed here?

EMMA

What?

JERRY

Wasn't it?

45

EMMA

We bought the bed. We bought everything. We bought the bed together.

JERRY

Ah. Yes.

EMMA *stands*.

EMMA

You'll make all the arrangements, then? With Mrs Banks?

Pause.

I don't want anything. Nowhere I can put it, you see. I have a home, with tablecloths and all the rest of it.

JERRY

I'll go into it, with Mrs Banks. There'll be a few quid, you know, so . . .

EMMA

No, I don't want any *cash*, thank you very much.

Silence. She puts coat on.

I'm going now.

He turns, looks at her.

Oh here's my key.

46

Takes out keyring, tries to take key from ring.

Oh Christ.

Struggles to take key from ring.
Throws him the ring.

You take it off.

He catches it, looks at her.

Can you just do it please? I'm picking up Charlotte
from school. I'm taking her shopping.

He takes key off.

Do you realise this is an afternoon? It's the Gallery's
afternoon off. That's why I'm here. We close every
Thursday afternoon. Can I have my keyring?

He gives it to her.

Thanks. Listen. I think we've made absolutely the right
decision.

She goes.

He stands.

1974

SCENE FOUR

Robert and Emma's House. Living room. 1974.
Autumn.

ROBERT *pouring a drink for* JERRY. *He goes to the*
door.

ROBERT

Emma! Jerry's here!

EMMA *(off)*

Who?

ROBERT

Jerry.

EMMA

I'll be down.

ROBERT *gives the drink to* JERRY.

JERRY

Cheers.

ROBERT

Cheers. She's just putting Ned to bed. I should think
he'll be off in a minute.

JERRY

Off where?

48

ROBERT

Dreamland.

JERRY

Ah. Yes, how is your sleep these days?

ROBERT

What?

JERRY

Do you still have bad nights? With Ned, I mean?

ROBERT

Oh, I see. Well, no. No, it's getting better. But you know what they say?

JERRY

What?

ROBERT

They say boys are worse than girls.

JERRY

Worse?

ROBERT

Babies. They say boy babies cry more than girl babies.

JERRY

Do they?

ROBERT

You didn't find that to be the case?

49

JERRY

Uh . . . yes, I think we did. Did you?

ROBERT

Yes. What do you make of it? Why do you think that
is?

JERRY

Well, I suppose . . . boys are more anxious.

ROBERT

Boy babies?

JERRY

Yes.

ROBERT

What the hell are they anxious about . . . at their age?
Do you think?

JERRY

Well . . . facing the world, I suppose, leaving the womb,
all that.

ROBERT

But what about girl babies? They leave the womb too.

JERRY

That's true. It's also true that nobody talks much about
girl babies leaving the womb. Do they?

ROBERT

I am prepared to do so.

JERRY

I see. Well, what have you got to say?

ROBERT

I was asking you a question.

JERRY

What was it?

ROBERT

Why do you assert that boy babies find leaving the womb more of a problem than girl babies?

JERRY

Have I made such an assertion?

ROBERT

You went on to make a further assertion, to the effect that boy babies are more anxious about facing the world than girl babies.

JERRY

Do you yourself believe that to be the case?

ROBERT

I do, yes.

Pause.

JERRY

Why do you think it is?

ROBERT

I have no answer.

Pause.

JERRY

Do you think it might have something to do with the difference between the sexes?

Pause.

ROBERT

Good God, you're right. That must be it.

EMMA *comes in.*

EMMA

Hullo. Surprise.

JERRY

I was having tea with Casey.

EMMA

Where?

JERRY

Just around the corner.

EMMA

I thought he lived in . . . Hampstead or somewhere.

ROBERT

You're out of date.

52

EMMA

Am I?

JERRY

He's left Susannah. He's living alone round the corner.

EMMA

Oh.

ROBERT

Writing a novel about a man who leaves his wife and three children and goes to live alone on the other side of London to write a novel about a man who leaves his wife and three children –

EMMA

I hope it's better than the last one.

ROBERT

The last one? Ah, the last one. Wasn't that the one about the man who lived in a big house in Hampstead with his wife and three children and is writing a novel about – ?

JERRY (*to* EMMA)

Why didn't you like it?

EMMA

I've told you actually.

JERRY

I think it's the best thing he's written.

EMMA

It may be the best thing he's *written* but it's still bloody dishonest.

JERRY

Dishonest? In what way dishonest?

EMMA

I've told you, actually.

JERRY

Have you?

ROBERT

Yes, she has. Once when we were all having dinner, I remember, you, me, Emma and Judith, where was it, Emma gave a dissertation over the pudding about dishonesty in Casey with reference to his last novel. 'Drying Out.' It was most stimulating. Judith had to leave unfortunately in the middle of it for her night shift at the hospital. How is Judith, by the way?

JERRY

Very well.

Pause.

ROBERT

When are we going to play squash?

JERRY

You're too good.

54

ROBERT

Not at all. I'm not good at all. I'm just fitter than you.

JERRY

But why? Why are you fitter than me?

ROBERT

Because I play squash.

JERRY

Oh, you're playing? Regularly?

ROBERT

Mmnn.

JERRY

With whom?

ROBERT

Casey, actually.

JERRY

Casey? Good Lord. What's he like?

ROBERT

He's a brutally honest squash player. No, really, we haven't played for years. We must play. You were rather good.

JERRY

Yes, I was quite good. All right. I'll give you a ring.

ROBERT

Why don't you?

JERRY

We'll make a date.

ROBERT

Right.

JERRY

Yes. We must do that.

ROBERT

And then I'll take you to lunch.

JERRY

No, no. I'll take you to lunch.

ROBERT

The man who wins buys the lunch.

EMMA

Can I watch?

Pause.

ROBERT

What?

EMMA

Why can't I watch and then take you both to lunch?

ROBERT

Well, to be brutally honest, we wouldn't actually want a
woman around, would we, Jerry? I mean a game of
squash isn't simply a game of squash, it's rather more
than that. You see, first there's the game. And then
there's the shower. And then there's the pint. And then
there's lunch. After all, you've been at it. You've had
your battle. What you want is your pint and your
lunch. You really don't want a woman buying you
lunch. You don't actually want a woman within a mile
of the place, any of the places, really. You don't want
her in the squash court, you don't want her in the
shower, or the pub, or the restaurant. You see, at lunch
you want to talk about squash, or cricket, or books, or
even women, with your friend, and be able to warm to
your theme without fear of improper interruption.
That's what it's all about. What do you think, Jerry?

JERRY

I haven't played squash for years.

Pause.

ROBERT

Well, let's play next week.

JERRY

I can't next week. I'm in New York.

EMMA

Are you?

JERRY

I'm going over with one of my more celebrated writers,
actually.

EMMA

Who?

JERRY

Casey. Someone wants to film that novel of his you
didn't like. We're going over to discuss it. It was a
question of them coming over here or us going over
there. Casey thought he deserved the trip.

EMMA

What about you?

JERRY

What?

EMMA

Do you deserve the trip?

ROBERT

Judith going?

JERRY

No. He can't go alone. We'll have that game of squash
when I get back. A week, or at the most ten days.

ROBERT

Lovely.

JERRY (*to* EMMA)

Bye.

ROBERT *and* JERRY *leave.*

She remains still.

ROBERT *returns. He kisses her. She responds. She breaks away, puts her head on his shoulder, cries quietly. He holds her.*

1973

SCENE FIVE
Hotel Room. Venice. 1973. Summer.

EMMA *on bed reading.* ROBERT *at window looking out.*
She looks up at him, then back at the book.

EMMA

It's Torcello tomorrow, isn't it?

ROBERT

What?

EMMA

We're going to Torcello tomorrow, aren't we?

ROBERT

Yes. That's right.

EMMA

That'll be lovely.

ROBERT

Mmn.

EMMA

I can't wait.

Pause.

ROBERT

Book good?

EMMA

Mmn. Yes.

ROBERT

What is it?

EMMA

This new book. This man Spinks.

ROBERT

Oh that. Jerry was telling me about it.

EMMA

Jerry? Was he?

ROBERT

He was telling me about it at lunch last week.

EMMA

Really? Does he like it?

ROBERT

Spinks is his boy. He discovered him.

EMMA

Oh. I didn't know that.

ROBERT

Unsolicited manuscript.

Pause.

You think it's good, do you?

EMMA

Yes, I do. I'm enjoying it.

ROBERT

Jerry thinks it's good too. You should have lunch with us one day and chat about it.

EMMA

Is that absolutely necessary?

Pause.

It's not as good as all that.

ROBERT

You mean it's not good enough for you to have lunch with Jerry and me and chat about it?

EMMA

What the hell are you talking about?

ROBERT

I must read it again myself, now it's in hard covers.

EMMA

Again?

ROBERT

Jerry wanted us to publish it.

62

EMMA

Oh, really?

ROBERT

Well, naturally. Anyway, I turned it down.

EMMA

Why?

ROBERT

Oh . . . not much more to say on that subject, really, is there?

EMMA

What do you consider the subject to be?

ROBERT

Betrayal.

EMMA

No, it isn't.

ROBERT

Isn't it? What is it then?

EMMA

I haven't finished it yet. I'll let you know.

ROBERT

Well, do let me know.

Pause.

Of course, I could be thinking of the wrong book.

Silence.

By the way, I went into American Express yesterday.

She looks up.

EMMA

Oh?

ROBERT

Yes. I went to cash some travellers cheques. You get a much better rate there, you see, than you do in an hotel.

EMMA

Oh, do you?

ROBERT

Oh yes. Anyway, there was a letter there for you. They asked me if you were any relation and I said yes. So they asked me if I wanted to take it. I mean, they gave it to me. But I said no, I would leave it. Did you get it?

EMMA

Yes.

ROBERT

I suppose you popped in when you were out shopping yesterday evening?

EMMA

That's right.

64

ROBERT

Oh well, I'm glad you got it.

Pause.

To be honest, I was amazed that they suggested I take it. It could never happen in England. But these Italians . . . so free and easy. I mean, just because my name is Downs and your name is Downs doesn't mean that we're the Mr and Mrs Downs that they, in their laughing Mediterranean way, assume we are. We could be, and in fact are vastly more likely to be, total strangers. So let's say I, whom they laughingly assume to be your husband, had taken the letter, having declared myself to be your husband but in truth being a total stranger, and opened it, and read it, out of nothing more than idle curiosity, and then thrown it in a canal, you would never have received it and would have been deprived of your legal right to open your own mail, and all this because of Venetian je m'en foutisme. I've a good mind to write to the Doge of Venice about it.

Pause.

That's what stopped me taking it, by the way, and bringing it to you, the thought that I could very easily be a total stranger.

Pause.

What they of course did not know, and had no way of knowing, was that I am your husband.

EMMA

Pretty inefficient bunch.

ROBERT

Only in a laughing Mediterranean way.

Pause.

EMMA

It was from Jerry.

ROBERT

Yes, I recognised the handwriting.

Pause.

How is he?

EMMA

Okay.

ROBERT

Good. And Judith?

EMMA

Fine.

Pause.

ROBERT

What about the kids?

EMMA

I don't think he mentioned them.

ROBERT

They're probably all right, then. If they were ill or
something he'd have probably mentioned it.

Pause.

Any other news?

EMMA

No.

Silence.

ROBERT

Are you looking forward to Torcello?

Pause.

How many times have we been to Torcello? Twice. I
remember how you loved it, the first time I took you
there. You fell in love with it. That was about ten years
ago, wasn't it? About . . . six months after we were
married. Yes. Do you remember? I wonder if you'll like
it as much tomorrow.

Pause.

What do you think of Jerry as a letter writer?

She laughs shortly.

You're trembling. Are you cold?

ROBERT's line continues above. Below:

EMMA

No.

ROBERT

He used to write to me at one time. Long letters about
Ford Madox Ford. I used to write to him too, come to
think of it. Long letters about . . . oh, W. B. Yeats, I
suppose. That was the time when we were both editors
of poetry magazines. Him at Cambridge, me at Oxford.
Did you know that? We were bright young men. And
close friends. Well, we still are close friends. All that
was long before I met you. Long before he met you. I've
been trying to remember when I introduced him to you.
I simply can't remember. I take it I *did* introduce him to
you? Yes. But when? Can you remember?

EMMA

No.

ROBERT

You can't?

EMMA

No.

ROBERT

How odd.

Pause.

He wasn't best man at our wedding, was he?

EMMA

You know he was.

ROBERT

Ah yes. Well, that's probably when I introduced him to you.

Pause.

Was there any message for me, in his letter?

Pause.

I mean in the line of business, to do with the world of publishing. Has he discovered any new and original talent? He's quite talented at uncovering talent, old Jerry.

EMMA

No message.

ROBERT

No message. Not even his love?

Silence.

EMMA

We're lovers.

ROBERT

Ah. Yes. I thought it might be something like that, something along those lines.

EMMA

When?

ROBERT

What?

EMMA

When did you think?

ROBERT

Yesterday. Only yesterday. When I saw his handwriting
on the letter. Before yesterday I was quite ignorant.

EMMA

Ah.

Pause.

I'm sorry.

ROBERT

Sorry?

Silence.

Where does it . . . take place? Must be a bit awkward. I
mean we've got two kids, he's got two kids, not to
mention a wife . . .

EMMA

We have a flat.

ROBERT

Ah. I see.

Pause.

Nice?

Pause.

A flat. It's quite well established then, your . . . uh . . . affair?

EMMA

Yes.

ROBERT

How long?

EMMA

Some time.

ROBERT

Yes, but how long exactly?

EMMA

Five years.

ROBERT

Five years?

Pause.

Ned is one year old.

Pause.

Did you hear what I said?

EMMA

Yes. He's your son. Jerry was in America. For two
months.

Silence.

ROBERT

Did he write to you from America?

EMMA

Of course. And I wrote to him.

ROBERT

Did you tell him that Ned had been conceived?

EMMA

Not by letter.

ROBERT

But when you did tell him, was he happy to know I was
to be a father?

Pause.

I've always liked Jerry. To be honest, I've always liked
him rather more than I've liked you. Maybe I should
have had an affair with him myself.

72

Silence.

Tell me, are you looking forward to our trip to
Torcello?

1973 Later

SCENE SIX
Flat. 1973. Summer.

EMMA *and* JERRY *standing, kissing. She is holding a
basket and a parcel.*

EMMA

Darling.

JERRY

Darling.

He continues to hold her. She laughs.

EMMA

I must put this down.

She puts basket on table.

JERRY

What's in it?

EMMA

Lunch.

JERRY

What?

EMMA

Things you like.

He pours wine.

How do I look?

JERRY

Beautiful.

EMMA

Do I look well?

JERRY

You do.

He gives her wine.

EMMA (*sipping*)

Mmmnn.

JERRY

How was it?

EMMA

It was lovely.

JERRY

Did you go to Torcello?

EMMA

No.

JERRY

Why not?

EMMA

Oh, I don't know. The speedboats were on strike, or something.

JERRY

On strike?

EMMA

Yes. On the day we were going.

JERRY

Ah. What about the gondolas?

EMMA

You can't take a gondola to Torcello.

JERRY

Well, they used to in the old days, didn't they? Before they had speedboats. How do you think they got over there?

EMMA

It would take hours.

JERRY

Yes. I suppose so.

Pause.

I got your letter.

EMMA

Good.

JERRY

Get mine?

EMMA

Of course. Miss me?

JERRY

Yes. Actually, I haven't been well.

EMMA

What?

JERRY

Oh nothing. A bug.

She kisses him.

EMMA

I missed you.

She turns away, looks about.

You haven't been here . . . at all?

JERRY

No.

EMMA

Needs hoovering.

JERRY

Later.

Pause.

I spoke to Robert this morning.

EMMA

Oh?

JERRY

I'm taking him to lunch on Thursday.

EMMA

Thursday? Why?

JERRY

Well, it's my turn.

EMMA

No, I meant why are you taking him to lunch?

JERRY

Because it's my turn. Last time he took me to lunch.

EMMA

You know what I mean.

JERRY

No. What?

EMMA

What is the subject or point of your lunch?

JERRY

No subject or point. We've just been doing it for years. His turn, followed by my turn.

EMMA

You've misunderstood me.

JERRY

Have I? How?

EMMA

Well, quite simply, you often do meet, or have lunch, to discuss a particular writer or a particular book, don't you? So to those meetings, or lunches, there is a point or a subject.

JERRY

Well, there isn't to this one.

Pause.

EMMA

You haven't discovered any new writers, while I've been away?

JERRY

No. Sam fell off his bike.

EMMA

No.

JERRY

He was knocked out. He was out for about a minute.

79

EMMA

Were you with him?

JERRY

No. Judith. He's all right. And then I got this bug.

EMMA

Oh dear.

JERRY

So I've had time for nothing.

EMMA

Everything will be better, now I'm back.

JERRY

Yes.

EMMA

Oh, I read that Spinks, the book you gave me.

JERRY

What do you think?

EMMA

Excellent.

JERRY

Robert hated it. He wouldn't publish it.

EMMA

What's he like?

JERRY

Who?

EMMA

Spinks.

JERRY

Spinks? He's a very thin bloke. About fifty. Wears dark glasses day and night. He lives alone, in a furnished room. Quite like this one, actually. He's . . . unfussed.

EMMA

Furnished rooms suit him?

JERRY

Yes.

EMMA

They suit me too. And you? Do you still like it? Our home?

JERRY

It's marvellous not to have a telephone.

EMMA

And marvellous to have me?

JERRY

You're all right.

EMMA

I cook and slave for you.

JERRY

You do.

EMMA

I bought something in Venice – for the house.

She opens the parcel, takes out a tablecloth. Puts it on the table.

Do you like it?

JERRY

It's lovely.

Pause.

EMMA

Do you think we'll ever go to Venice together?

Pause.

No. Probably not.

Pause.

JERRY

You don't think I should see Robert for lunch on Thursday, or on Friday, for that matter?

EMMA

Why do you say that?

JERRY

You don't think I should see him at all?

EMMA

I didn't say that. How can you not see him? Don't be silly.

Pause.

JERRY

I had a terrible panic when you were away. I was sorting out a contract, in my office, with some lawyers. I suddenly couldn't remember what I'd done with your letter. I couldn't remember putting it in the safe. I said I had to look for something in the safe. I opened the safe. It wasn't there. I had to go on with the damn contract . . . I kept seeing it lying somewhere in the house, being picked up . . .

EMMA

Did you find it?

JERRY

It was in the pocket of a jacket – in my wardrobe – at home.

EMMA

God.

JERRY

Something else happened a few months ago – I didn't tell you. We had a drink one evening. Well, we had our drink, and I got home about eight, walked in the door,

Judith said, hello, you're a bit late. Sorry, I said, I was
having a drink with Spinks. Spinks? she said, how odd,
he's just phoned, five minutes ago, wanted to speak to
you, he didn't mention he'd just seen you. You know
old Spinks, I said, not exactly forthcoming, is he? He'd
probably remembered something he'd meant to say but
hadn't. I'll ring him later. I went up to see the kids and
then we all had dinner.

Pause.

Listen. Do you remember, when was it, a few years ago,
we were all in your kitchen, must have been Christmas
or something, do you remember, all the kids were
running about and suddenly I picked Charlotte up and
lifted her high up, high up, and then down and up. Do
you remember how she laughed?

EMMA

Everyone laughed.

JERRY

She was so light. And there was your husband and my
wife and all the kids, all standing and laughing in your
kitchen. I can't get rid of it.

EMMA

It was your kitchen, actually.

*He takes her hand. They stand. They go to the bed and
lie down.*

84

Why shouldn't you throw her up?

She caresses him. They embrace.

1973 Later

SCENE SEVEN
Restaurant. 1973. Summer.

ROBERT *at table drinking white wine. The* WAITER *brings* JERRY *to the table.* JERRY *sits.*

JERRY

Hullo, Robert.

ROBERT

Hullo.

JERRY (*to the* WAITER)

I'd like a Scotch on the rocks.

WAITER

With water?

JERRY

What?

WAITER

You want it with water?

JERRY

No. No water. Just on the rocks.

WAITER

Certainly signore.

86

ROBERT

Scotch? You don't usually drink Scotch at lunchtime.

JERRY

I've had a bug, actually.

ROBERT

Ah.

JERRY

And the only thing to get rid of this bug was Scotch – at lunchtime as well as at night. So I'm still drinking Scotch at lunchtime in case it comes back.

ROBERT

Like an apple a day.

JERRY

Precisely.

WAITER *brings Scotch on rocks.*

Cheers.

ROBERT

Cheers.

WAITER

The menus, signori.

He passes the menus, goes.

ROBERT

How are you? Apart from the bug?

JERRY

Fine.

ROBERT

Ready for some squash?

JERRY

When I've got rid of the bug, yes.

ROBERT

I thought you had got rid of it.

JERRY

Why do you think I'm still drinking Scotch at
lunchtime?

ROBERT

Oh yes. We really must play. We haven't played for
years.

JERRY

How old are you now, then?

ROBERT

Thirty-six.

JERRY

That means I'm thirty-six as well.

88

ROBERT

If you're a day.

JERRY

Bit violent, squash.

ROBERT

Ring me. We'll have a game.

JERRY

How was Venice?

WAITER

Ready to order, signori?

ROBERT

What'll you have?

JERRY *looks at him, briefly, then back to the menu.*

JERRY

I'll have melone. And Piccata al limone with a green
salad.

WAITER

Insalate verde. Prosciutto e melone?

JERRY

No. Just melone. On the rocks.

ROBERT

I'll have prosciutto and melone. Fried scampi. And
spinach.

WAITER

E spinaci. Grazie, signore.

ROBERT

And a bottle of Corvo Bianco straight away.

WAITER

Si, signore. Molte grazies. (*He goes.*)

JERRY

Is he the one who's always been here or is it his son?

ROBERT

You mean has his son always been here?

JERRY

No, is *he* his son? I mean, is he the son of the one who's always been here?

ROBERT

No, he's his father.

JERRY

Ah. Is he?

ROBERT

He's the one who speaks wonderful Italian.

JERRY

Yes. Your Italian's pretty good, isn't it?

ROBERT

No. Not at all.

JERRY

Yes it is.

ROBERT

No, it's Emma's Italian which is very good. Emma's Italian is very good.

JERRY

Is it? I didn't know that.

WAITER *with bottle.*

WAITER

Corvo Bianco, signore.

ROBERT

Thank you.

JERRY

How was it, anyway? Venice.

WAITER

Venice, signore? Beautiful. A most beautiful place of Italy. You see that painting on the wall? Is Venice.

ROBERT

So it is.

WAITER

You know what is none of in Venice?

JERRY

What?

WAITER

Traffico.

He goes, smiling.

ROBERT

Cheers.

JERRY

Cheers.

ROBERT

When were you last there?

JERRY

Oh, years.

ROBERT

How's Judith?

JERRY

What? Oh, you know, okay. Busy.

ROBERT

And the kids?

JERRY

All right. Sam fell off –

ROBERT

What?

JERRY

No, no, nothing. So how was it?

ROBERT

You used to go there with Judith, didn't you?

JERRY

Yes, but we haven't been there for years.

Pause.

How about Charlotte? Did she enjoy it?

ROBERT

I think she did.

Pause.

I did.

JERRY

Good.

ROBERT

I went for a trip to Torcello.

JERRY

Oh, really? Lovely place.

ROBERT

Incredible day. I got up very early and – whoomp –
right across the lagoon – to Torcello. Not a soul
stirring.

JERRY

What's the 'whoomp'?

ROBERT

Speedboat.

JERRY

Ah. I thought –

ROBERT

What?

JERRY

It's so long ago, I'm obviously wrong. I thought one
went to Torcello by gondola.

ROBERT

It would take hours. No, no, – whoomp – across the
lagoon in the dawn.

JERRY

Sounds good.

ROBERT

I was quite alone.

JERRY

Where was Emma?

ROBERT

I think asleep.

94

JERRY

Ah.

ROBERT

I was alone for hours, as a matter of fact, on the island.
Highpoint, actually, of the whole trip.

JERRY

Was it? Well, it sounds marvellous.

ROBERT

Yes. I sat on the grass and read Yeats.

JERRY

Yeats on Torcello?

ROBERT

They went well together.

WAITER *with food.*

WAITER

One melone. One prosciutto e melone.

ROBERT

Prosciutto for me.

WAITER

Buon appetito.

ROBERT

Emma read that novel of that chum of yours – what's
his name?

95

JERRY

I don't know. What?

ROBERT

Spinks.

JERRY

Oh Spinks. Yes. The one you didn't like.

ROBERT

The one I wouldn't publish.

JERRY

I remember. Did Emma like it?

ROBERT

She seemed to be madly in love with it.

JERRY

Good.

ROBERT

You like it yourself, do you?

JERRY

I do.

ROBERT

And it's very successful?

JERRY

It is.

ROBERT

Tell me, do you think that makes me a publisher of
unique critical judgement or a foolish publisher?

JERRY

A foolish publisher.

ROBERT

I agree with you. I am a very foolish publisher.

JERRY

No you're not. What are you talking about? You're a
good publisher. What are you talking about?

ROBERT

I'm a bad publisher because I hate books. Or to be more
precise, prose. Or to be even more precise, modern
prose, I mean modern novels, first novels and second
novels, all that promise and sensibility it falls upon me
to judge, to put the firm's money on, and then to push
for the third novel, see it done, see the dust jacket done,
see the dinner for the national literary editors done, see
the signing in Hatchards done, see the lucky author
cook himself to death, all in the name of literature. You
know what you and Emma have in common? You love
literature. I mean you love modern prose literature, I
mean you love the new novel by the new Casey or
Spinks. It gives you both a thrill.

JERRY

You must be pissed.

ROBERT

Really? You mean you don't think it gives Emma a thrill?

JERRY

How do I know? She's your wife.

Pause.

ROBERT

Yes. Yes. You're quite right. I shouldn't have to consult you. I shouldn't have to consult anyone.

JERRY

I'd like some more wine.

ROBERT

Yes, yes. Waiter! Another bottle of Corvo Bianco. And where's our lunch? This place is going to pot. Mind you, it's worse in Venice. They really don't give a fuck there. I'm not drunk. You can't get drunk on Corvo Bianco. Mind you . . . last night . . . I was up late . . . I hate brandy . . . it stinks of modern literature. No, look, I'm sorry . . .

WAITER *with bottle.*

WAITER

Corvo Bianco.

ROBERT

Same glass. Where's our lunch?

WAITER

It comes.

ROBERT

I'll pour.

WAITER *goes, with melon plates.*

No, look, I'm sorry, have another drink. I'll tell you what it is, it's just that I can't bear being back in London. I was happy, such a rare thing, not in Venice, I don't mean that, I mean on Torcello, when I walked about Torcello in the early morning, alone, I was happy, I wanted to stay there for ever.

JERRY

We all . . .

ROBERT

Yes, we all . . . feel that sometimes. Oh you do yourself, do you?

Pause.

I mean there's nothing really wrong, you see. I've got the family. Emma and I are very good together. I think the world of her. And I actually consider Casey to be a first-rate writer.

JERRY

Do you really?

ROBERT

First rate. I'm proud to publish him and you discovered
him and that was very clever of you.

JERRY

Thanks.

ROBERT

You've got a good nose and you care and I respect that
in you. So does Emma. We often talk about it.

JERRY

How is Emma?

ROBERT

Very well. You must come and have a drink sometime.
She'd love to see you.

1971

SCENE EIGHT
Flat. 1971. Summer.

Flat empty. Kitchen door open. Table set; crockery, glasses, bottle of wine.

JERRY *comes in through front door, with key.*

JERRY
Hullo.

EMMA's *voice from kitchen.*

EMMA
Hullo.

EMMA *comes out of kitchen. She is wearing an apron.*

EMMA
I've only just got here. I meant to be here ages ago. I'm making this stew. It'll be hours.

He kisses her.

Are you starving?

JERRY
Yes.

He kisses her.

EMMA

No really. I'll never do it. You sit down. I'll get it on.

JERRY

What a lovely apron.

EMMA

Good.

She kisses him, goes into kitchen.
She calls. He pours wine.

EMMA

What have you been doing?

JERRY

Just walked through the park.

EMMA

What was it like?

JERRY

Beautiful. Empty. A slight mist.

Pause.

I sat down for a bit, under a tree. It was very quiet. I just looked at the Serpentine.

Pause.

EMMA

And then?

JERRY

Then I got a taxi to Wessex Grove. Number 31. And I climbed the steps and opened the front door and then climbed the stairs and opened this door and found you in a new apron cooking a stew.

EMMA *comes out of the kitchen.*

EMMA

It's on.

JERRY

Which is now on.

EMMA *pours herself a vodka.*

JERRY

Vodka? At lunchtime?

EMMA

Just feel like one.

She drinks.

I ran into Judith yesterday. Did she tell you?

JERRY

No, she didn't.

Pause.

Where?

EMMA

Lunch.

JERRY

Lunch?

EMMA

She didn't tell you?

JERRY

No.

EMMA

That's funny.

JERRY

What do you mean, lunch? Where?

EMMA

At Fortnum and Mason's.

JERRY

Fortnum and Mason's? What the hell was she doing at
Fortnum and Mason's?

EMMA

She was lunching with a lady.

JERRY

A lady?

EMMA

Yes.

Pause.

JERRY

Fortnum and Mason's is a long way from the hospital.

EMMA

Of course it isn't.

JERRY

Well . . . I suppose not.

Pause.

And you?

EMMA

Me?

JERRY

What were you doing at Fortnum and Mason's?

EMMA

Lunching with my sister.

JERRY

Ah.

Pause.

EMMA

Judith . . . didn't tell you?

JERRY

I haven't really seen her. I was out late last night, with Casey. And she was out early this morning.

Pause.

EMMA

Do you think she knows?

JERRY

Knows?

EMMA

Does she know? About us?

JERRY

No.

EMMA

Are you sure?

JERRY

She's too busy. At the hospital. And then the kids. She doesn't go in for . . . speculation.

EMMA

But what about clues? Isn't she interested . . . to follow clues?

JERRY

What clues?

EMMA

Well, there must be some . . . available to her . . . to
pick up.

JERRY

There are none . . . available to her.

EMMA

Oh. Well . . . good.

JERRY

She has an admirer.

EMMA

Really?

JERRY

Another doctor. He takes her for drinks. It's . . .
irritating. I mean, she says that's all there is to it. He
likes her, she's fond of him, et cetera, et cetera . . .
perhaps that's what I find irritating. I don't know
exactly what's going on.

EMMA

Oh, why shouldn't she have an admirer? I have an
admirer.

JERRY

Who?

EMMA

Uuh . . . you, I think.

JERRY

Ah. Yes.

He takes her hand.

I'm more than that.

Pause.

EMMA

Tell me . . . have you ever thought . . . of changing your life?

JERRY

Changing?

EMMA

Mmnn.

Pause.

JERRY

It's impossible.

Pause.

EMMA

Do you think she's being unfaithful to you?

JERRY

No. I don't know.

EMMA

When you were in America, just now, for instance?

JERRY

No.

EMMA

Have you ever been unfaithful?

JERRY

To whom?

EMMA

To me, of course.

JERRY

No.

Pause.

Have you . . . to me?

EMMA

No.

Pause.

If she was, what would you do?

JERRY

She isn't. She's busy. She's got lots to do. She's a very good doctor. She likes her life. She loves the kids.

EMMA

Ah.

JERRY

She loves me.

Pause.

EMMA

Ah.

Silence.

JERRY

All that means something.

EMMA

It certainly does.

JERRY

But I adore you.

Pause.

I adore you.

EMMA *takes his hand.*

EMMA

Yes.

Pause.

Listen. There's something I have to tell you.

JERRY

What?

EMMA

I'm pregnant. It was when you were in America.

Pause.

It wasn't anyone else. It was my husband.

Pause.

JERRY

Yes. Yes, of course.

Pause.

I'm very happy for you.

1968

SCENE NINE
Robert and Emma's House. Bedroom. 1968. Winter.

The room is dimly lit. JERRY *is sitting in the shadows. Faint music through the door.*

The door opens. Light. Music. EMMA *comes in, closes the door. She goes towards the mirror, sees* JERRY.

EMMA

Good God.

JERRY

I've been waiting for you.

EMMA

What do you mean?

JERRY

I knew you'd come.

He drinks.

EMMA

I've just come in to comb my hair.

He stands.

JERRY

I knew you'd have to. I knew you'd have to comb your

hair. I knew you'd have to get away from the party.

She goes to the mirror, combs her hair.
He watches her.

You're a beautiful hostess.

EMMA
Aren't you enjoying the party?

JERRY
You're beautiful.

He goes to her.

Listen. I've been watching you all night. I must tell you,
I want to tell you, I have to tell you –

EMMA
Please –

JERRY
You're incredible.

EMMA
You're drunk.

JERRY
Nevertheless.

He holds her.

EMMA

Jerry.

JERRY

I was best man at your wedding. I saw you in white. I watched you glide by in white.

EMMA

I wasn't in white.

JERRY

You know what should have happened?

EMMA

What?

JERRY

I should have had you, in your white, before the wedding. I should have blackened you, in your white wedding dress, blackened you in your bridal dress, before ushering you into your wedding, as your best man.

EMMA

My husband's best man. Your best friend's best man.

JERRY

No. Your best man.

EMMA

I must get back.

JERRY

You're lovely. I'm crazy about you. All these words I'm
using, don't you see, they've never been said before.
Can't you see? I'm crazy about you. It's a whirlwind.
Have you ever been to the Sahara Desert? Listen to me.
It's true. Listen. You overwhelm me. You're so lovely.

EMMA

I'm not.

JERRY

You're so beautiful. Look at the way you look at me.

EMMA

I'm not . . . looking at you.

JERRY

Look at the way you're looking at me. I can't wait for
you, I'm bowled over, I'm totally knocked out, you
dazzle me, you jewel, my jewel, I can't ever sleep again,
no, listen, it's the truth, I won't walk, I'll be a cripple,
I'll descend, I'll diminish, into total paralysis, my life is
in your hands, that's what you're banishing me to, a
state of catatonia, do you know the state of catatonia?
do you? do you? the state of . . . where the reigning
prince is the prince of emptiness, the prince of absence,
the prince of desolation. I love you.

EMMA

My husband is at the other side of that door.

JERRY

Everyone knows. The world knows. It knows. But

they'll never know, they'll never know, they're in a different world. I adore you. I'm madly in love with you. I can't believe that what anyone is at this moment saying has ever happened has ever happened. Nothing has ever happened. Nothing. This is the only thing that has ever happened. Your eyes kill me. I'm lost. You're wonderful.

EMMA

No.

JERRY

Yes.

He kisses her.
She breaks away.
He kisses her.

Laughter off.
She breaks away.
Door opens. ROBERT.

EMMA

Your best friend is drunk.

JERRY

As you are my best and oldest friend and, in the present instance, my host, I decided to take this opportunity to tell your wife how beautiful she was.

ROBERT

Quite right.

JERRY

It is quite right, to . . . to face up to the facts . . . and to offer a token, without blush, a token of one's unalloyed appreciation, no holds barred.

ROBERT

Absolutely.

JERRY

And how wonderful for you that this is so, that this is the case, that her beauty is the case.

ROBERT

Quite right.

JERRY *moves to* ROBERT *and take hold of his elbow.*

JERRY

I speak as your oldest friend. Your best man.

ROBERT

You are, actually.

He clasps JERRY's *shoulder, briefly, turns, leaves the room.*

EMMA *moves towards the door.* JERRY *grasps her arm. She stops still.*

They stand still, looking at each other.

MONOLOGUE

Monologue was first shown on BBC Television
on 13 April 1973.

MAN   Henry Woolf

Directed by Christopher Morahan

Man alone in a chair.
He refers to another chair, which is empty.

MAN
I think I'll nip down to the games room. Stretch my
legs. Have a game of ping pong. What about you?
Fancy a game? How would you like a categorical
thrashing? I'm willing to accept any challenge, any
stakes, any gauntlet you'd care to fling down. What
have you done with your gauntlets, by the way? In fact,
while we're at it, what happened to your motorbike?

Pause.

You looked bold in black. The only thing I didn't like
was your face, too white, the face, stuck between your
black helmet and your black hair and your black
motoring jacket, kind of aghast, blatantly vulnerable,
veering towards pitiful. Of course, you weren't cut out
to be a motorbikist, it went against your nature, I never
understood what you were getting at. What is certain is
that it didn't work, it never convinced me, it never got
you onto any top shelf with me. You should have been
black, you should have had a black face, then you'd be
getting somewhere, really making a go of it.

Pause.

121

I often had the impression . . . often . . . that you two
were actually brother and sister, some kind of link-up,
some kind of identical shimmer, deep down in your
characters, an inkling, no more, that at one time you
had shared the same pot. But of course she was black.
Black as the Ace of Spades. And a life-lover, to boot.

Pause.

All the same, you and I, even then, never mind the
weather, weren't we, we were always available for net
practice, at the drop of a hat, or a game of fives, or a
walk and talk through the park, or a couple of rounds
of putting before lunch, given fair to moderate
conditions, and no burdensome commitments.

Pause.

The thing I like, I mean quite immeasurably, is this kind
of conversation, this kind of exchange, this class of
mutual reminiscence.

Pause.

Sometimes I think you've forgotten the black girl, the
ebony one. Sometimes I think you've forgotten me.

Pause.

You haven't forgotten *me*. Who was your best mate,
who was your truest mate? You introduced me to
Webster and Tourneur, admitted, but who got you
going on Tristan Tzara, Breton, Giacometti and all that

122

lot? Not to mention Louis-Ferdinand Céline, now out of favour. And John Dos. Who bought you both all those custard tins cut price? I say both. I was the best friend either of you ever had and I'm still prepared to prove it, I'm still prepared to wrap my braces round anyone's neck, in your defence.

Pause.

Now you're going to say you loved her soul and I loved her body. You're going to trot that old one out. I know you were much more beautiful than me, much more *aquiline*, I know *that*, that I'll give you, more *ethereal*, more thoughtful, *slyer*, while I had both feet firmly planted on the deck. But I'll tell you one thing you don't know. She loved my soul. It was my soul she loved.

Pause.

You never say what you're ready for now. You're not even ready for a game of ping pong. You're incapable of saying of what it is you're capable, where your relish lies, where you're sharp, excited, why you never are capable . . . never are . . . capable of exercising a crisp and full-bodied appraisal of the buzzing possibilities of your buzzing brain cells. You often, I'll be frank, act as if you're dead, as if the Balls Pond Road and the lovely ebony lady never existed, as if the rain in the light on the pavements in the twilight never existed, as if our sporting and intellectual life never was.

Pause.

She was tired. She sat down. She was tired. The journey. The rush hour. The weather, so unpredictable. She'd put on a woollen dress because the morning was chilly, but the day had changed, totally, totally changed. She cried. You jumped up like a . . . those things, forgot the name, monkey on a box, *jack in a box*, held her hand, made her tea, a rare burst. Perhaps the change in the weather had gone to your head.

Pause.

I loved her body. Not that, between ourselves, it's one way or another a thing of any importance. My spasms could be your spasms. Who's to tell or care?

Pause.

Well . . . she did . . . can . . . could . . .

Pause.

We all walked, arm in arm, through the long grass, over the bridge, sat outside the pub in the sun by the river, the pub was shut.

Pause.

Did anyone notice us? Did you see anyone looking at us?

Pause.

Touch my body, she said to you. You did. Of course you

124

did. You'd be a bloody fool if you didn't. You'd have
been a bloody fool if you hadn't. It was perfectly
normal.

Pause.

That was behind the partition.

Pause.

I brought her to see you, after you'd pissed off to live in
Notting Hill Gate. Naturally. They all end up there. I'll
never end up there. I'll never end up on that side of the
Park.

Pause.

Sitting there with your record player, growing bald,
Beethoven, cocoa, cats. That really dates it. The cocoa
dates it. It was your detachment was dangerous. I knew
it of course like the back of my hand. That was the web
my darling black darling hovered in, wavered in, my
black *moth*. She stuttered in that light, your slightly
sullen, non-committal, deadly dangerous light. But it's a
fact of life. The ones that keep silent are the best off.

Pause.

As for me, I've always liked simple love scenes, the
classic set-ups, the sweet . . . the sweet . . . the sweet
farewell at Paddington Station. My collar turned up.
Her soft cheeks. Standing close to me, legs under her
raincoat, the platform, her cheeks, her hands, nothing

like the sound of steam to keep love warm, to keep it moist, to bring it to the throat, my ebony love, she smiles at me, I touched her.

Pause.

I feel for you. Even if you feel nothing . . . for me. I feel for you, old chap.

Pause.

I keep busy in the *mind*, and that's why I'm still sparking, get it? I've got a hundred per cent more energy in me now than when I was twenty-two. When I was twenty-two I slept twenty-four hours a day. And twenty-two hours a day at twenty-four. Work it out for yourself. But now I'm sparking, at my peak, *up here*, two thousand revolutions a second, every living hour of the day and night. I'm a front runner. My watchword is vigilance. I'm way past mythologies, left them all behind, cocoa, sleep, Beethoven, cats, rain, black girls, bosom pals, literature, custard. You'll say I've been talking about nothing else all night, but can't you see, you bloody fool, that I can *afford* to do it, can't you appreciate the irony? Even if you're too dim to catch the irony in the words themselves, the words I have chosen myself, quite scrupulously, and with intent, you can't miss the irony in the tone of *voice*!

Pause.

What you are in fact witnessing is freedom. I no longer participate in holy ceremony. The crap is cut.

Silence.

You should have had a black face, that was your mistake. You could have made a going concern out of it, you could have chalked it up in the book, you could have had two black kids.

Pause.

I'd have died for them.

Pause.

I'd have been their uncle.

Pause.

I am their uncle.

Pause.

I'm your children's uncle.

Pause.

I'll take them out, tell them jokes.

Pause.

I love your children.

FAMILY VOICES

Family Voices was first broadcast on BBC Radio 3 on 22 January 1981. The cast was as follows:

VOICE 1   Michael Kitchen
VOICE 2   Peggy Ashcroft
VOICE 3   Mark Dignam

Directed by Peter Hall

It was presented in a 'platform performance' by the National Theatre, London, on 13 February 1981. Cast and director were the same. The decor was by John Bury.

Family Voices was subsequently presented with *A Kind of Alaska* and *Victoria Station* as part of the triple bill, *Other Places*, first performed at the National Theatre, London, on 14 October 1982. The cast was as follows:

VOICE 1   Nigel Havers
VOICE 2   Anna Massey
VOICE 3   Paul Rogers

Directed by Peter Hall

I am having a very nice time.

The weather is up and down, but surprisingly warm, on the whole, more often than not.

I hope you're feeling well, and not as peaky as you did, the last time I saw you.

No, you didn't feel peaky, you felt perfectly well, you simply looked peaky.

Do you miss me?

I am having a very nice time and I hope you are glad of that.

At the moment I am dead drunk.

I had five pints in The Fishmongers Arms tonight, followed by three double Scotches, and literally rolled home.

When I say home I can assure you that my room is extremely pleasant. So is the bathroom. Extremely pleasant. I have some very pleasant baths indeed in the bathroom. So does everybody else in the house. They all lie quite naked in the bath and have very pleasant baths indeed. All the people in the house go about saying what a superb bath and bathroom the one we share is, they go about telling literally everyone they meet what lovely baths you can get in this place, more or less unparalleled, to put it bluntly.

It's got a lot to do with the landlady, who is a Mrs Withers, a person who turns out be an utterly charming person, of impeccable credentials.

When I said I was drunk I was of course making a joke.

I bet you laughed.

Mother?

Did you get the joke? You know I never touch alcohol.

I like being in this enormous city, all by myself. I expect to make friends in the not too distant future.

I expect to make girlfriends too.

I expect to meet a very nice girl. Having met her, I shall bring her home to meet my mother.

I like walking in this enormous city, all by myself. It's fun to know no one at all. When I pass people in the street they don't realise that I don't know them from Adam. They know other people and even more other people know them, so they naturally think that even if I don't know them I know the other people. So they look at me, they try to catch my eye, they expect me to speak. But as I do not know them I do not speak. Nor do I ever feel the slightest temptation to do so.

You see, mother, I am not lonely, because all that has ever happened to me is with me, keeps me company; my childhood, for example, through which you, my mother, and he, my father, guided me.

I get on very well with my landlady, Mrs Withers. She tells me I am her solace. I have a drink with her at lunchtime and another one at teatime and then take her for a couple in the evening at The Fishmongers Arms.

She was in the Women's Air Force in the Second World War. Don't drop a bollock, Charlie, she's fond of saying, Call him Flight Sergeant and he'll be happy as a pig in shit.

You'd really like her, mother.

I think it's dawn. I can see it coming up. Another day. A day I warmly welcome. And so I shall end this letter to you, my dear mother, with my love.

VOICE 2

Darling. Where are you? The flowers are wonderful here. The blooms. You so loved them. Why do you never write?

I think of you and wonder how you are. Do you ever think of me? Your mother? Ever? At all?

Have you changed your address?

133

Have you made friends with anyone? A nice boy? Or a nice girl?

There are so many nice boys and nice girls about. But please don't get mixed up with the other sort. They can land you in such terrible trouble. And you'd hate it so. You're so scrupulous, so particular.

I often think that I would love to live happily ever after with you and your young wife. And she would be such a lovely wife to you and I would have the occasional dinner with you both. A dinner I would be quite happy to cook myself, should you both be tired after your long day, as I'm sure you will be.

I sometimes walk the cliff path and think of you. I think of the times you walked the cliff path, with your father, with cheese sandwiches. Didn't you? You both sat on the clifftop and ate my cheese sandwiches together. Do you remember our little joke? Munch, munch. We had a damn good walk, your father would say. You mean you had a good munch munch, I would say. And you would both laugh.

Darling. I miss you. I gave birth to you. Where are you?

I wrote to you three months ago, telling you of your father's death. Did you receive my letter?

VOICE 1
I'm not at all sure that I like the people in this house, apart from Mrs Withers and her daughter, Jane. Jane is a schoolgirl who works hard at her homework.

She keeps her nose to the grindstone. This I find impressive. There's not too much of that about these days. But I'm not so sure about the other people in this house.

One is an old man.

The one who is an old man retires early. He is bald.

The other is a woman who wears red dresses.

The other one is another man.

He is big. He is much bigger than the other man. His hair is black. He has black eyebrows and black hair on the back of his hands.

I ask Mrs Withers about them but she will talk of nothing but her days in the Women's Air Force in the Second World War.

I have decided that Jane is not Mrs Withers' daughter but her grand-daughter. Mrs Withers is seventy. Jane is fifteen. That I am convinced is the truth.

At night I hear whispering from the other rooms and do not understand it. I hear steps on the stairs but do not dare go out to investigate.

VOICE 2

As your father grew closer to his death he spoke more and more of you, with tenderness and bewilderment. I consoled him with the idea that you had left home to

make him proud of you. I think I succeeded in this. One
of his last sentences was: Give him a slap on the back
from me. Give him a slap on the back from me.

VOICE 1

I have made a remarkable discovery. The old man who
is bald and who retires early is named Withers.
Benjamin Withers. Unless it is simply a coincidence it
must mean that he is a relation.

I asked Mrs Withers what the truth of this was. She
poured herself a gin and looked at it before she drank it.
Then she looked at me and said: You are my little pet.
I've always wanted a little pet but I've never had one
and now I've got one.

Sometimes she gives me a cuddle, as if she were my
mother.

But I haven't forgotten that I have a mother and that
you are my mother.

VOICE 2

Sometimes I wonder if you remember that you have a
mother.

VOICE 1

Something has happened. The woman who wears red
dresses stopped me and asked me into her room for a
cup of tea. I went into her room. It was far bigger than I
had expected, with sofas and curtains and veils and
shrouds and rugs and soft material all over the walls,
dark blue. Jane was sitting on a sofa doing her

homework, by the look of it. I was invited to sit on the
same sofa. Tea had already been made and stood ready,
in a china teaset, of a most elegant design. I was given a
cup. So was Jane, who smiled at me. I haven't
introduced myself, the woman said, my name is Lady
Withers. Jane sipped her tea with her legs up on the
sofa. Her stockinged toes came to rest on my thigh. It
wasn't the biggest sofa in the world. Lady Withers sat
opposite us on a substantially bigger sofa. Her dress, I
decided, wasn't red but pink. Jane was in green, apart
from her toes, which were clad in black. Lady Withers
asked me about you, mother. She asked me about my
mother. I said, with absolute conviction, that you were
the best mother in the world. She asked me to call her
Lally. And to call Jane Jane. I said I did call Jane Jane.
Jane gave me a bun. I think it was a bun. Lady Withers
bit into her bun. Jane bit into her bun, her toes now
resting on my lap. Lady Withers seemed to be enjoying
her bun, on her sofa. She finished it and picked up
another. I had never seen so many buns. One quick
glance told me they were perched on cakestands, all
over the room. Lady Withers went through her second
bun with no trouble at all and was at once on to
another. Jane, on the other hand, chewed almost
dreamily at her bun and when a currant was left
stranded on her upper lip she licked it off, without
haste. I could not reconcile this with the fact that her
toes were quite restless, even agitated. Her mouth,
eating, was measured, serene; her toes, not eating, were
agitated, highly strung, some would say hysterical. My
bun turned out to be rock solid. I bit into it, it jumped
out of my mouth and bounced into my lap. Jane's feet
caught it. It calmed her toes down. She juggled the bun,

with some expertise, along them. I recalled that, in an
early exchange between us, she had told me she wanted
to be an acrobat.

VOICE 2
Darling. Where are you? Why do you never write?
Nobody knows your whereabouts. Nobody knows if
you are alive or dead. Nobody can find you. Have you
changed your name?

If you are alive you are a monster. On his deathbed
your father cursed you. He cursed me too, to tell the
truth. He cursed everyone in sight. Except that you
were not in sight. I do not blame you entirely for your
father's ill humour, but your absence and silence were a
great burden on him, a weariness to him. He died in
lamentation and oath. Was that your wish? Now I am
alone, apart from Millie, who sometimes comes over
from Dover. She is some consolation. Her eyes well with
tears when she speaks of you, your dear sister's eyes
well with tears. She has made a truly happy marriage
and has a lovely little boy. When he is older he will
want to know where his uncle is. What shall we say?

Or perhaps you will arrive here in a handsome new car,
one day, in the not too distant future, in a nice new suit,
quite out of the blue, and hold me in your arms.

VOICE 1
Lady Withers stood up. As Jane is doing her homework,
she said, perhaps you would care to leave and come
again another day. Jane withdrew her feet, my bun
clasped between her two big toes. Yes of course, I said,

unless Jane would like me to help her with her
homework. No thank you, said Lady Withers, I shall
help her with her homework.

What I didn't say is that I am thinking of offering
myself out as a tutor. I consider that I would make an
excellent tutor, to the young, in any one of a number of
subjects. Jane would be an ideal pupil. She possesses a
true love of learning. That is the sense of her one takes
from her every breath, her every sigh and exhalation.
When she turns her eyes upon you you see within her
eyes, raw, untutored, unexercised but willing, a deep
love of learning.

These are midnight thoughts, mother, although the time
is ten twenty-three, precisely.

VOICE 2

Darling?

VOICE I

While I was lying in my bath this afternoon, thinking
on these things, there was apparently a knock on the
front door. The man with black hair apparently opened
the door. Two women stood on the doorstep. They said
they were my mother and my sister, and asked for me.
He denied knowledge of me. No, he had not heard of
me. No, there was no one of that name resident. This
was a family house, no strangers admitted. No, they got
on very well, thank you very much, without intruders. I
suggest, he said, that you both go back to where you
come from, and stop bothering innocent hardworking
people with your slanders and your libels, these all too

predictable excrescences of the depraved mind at the end of its tether. I can smell your sort a mile off and I am quite prepared to put you both on a charge of malicious mischief, insulting behaviour and vagabondage, in other words wandering around on doorsteps knowingly, without any visible means of support. So piss off out of it before I call a copper.

I was lying in my bath when the door opened. I thought I had locked it. My name's Riley, he said, How's the bath? Very nice, I said. You've got a wellknit yet slender frame, he said, I thought you only a snip, I never imagined you would be as wellknit and slender as I now see you are. Oh thank you, I said. Don't thank me, he said, It's God you have to thank. Or your mother. I've just dismissed a couple of imposters at the front door. We'll get no more shit from that quarter. He then sat on the edge of the bath and recounted to me what I've just recounted to you.

It interests me that my father wasn't bothered to make the trip.

VOICE 2

I hear your father's step on the stair. I hear his cough. But his step and his cough fade. He does not open the door.

Sometimes I think I have always been sitting like this. I sometimes think I have always been sitting like this, alone by an indifferent fire, curtains closed, night, winter.

You see, I have my thoughts too. Thoughts no one else knows I have, thoughts none of my family ever knew I had. But I write of them to you now, wherever you are.

What I mean is that when, for example, I was washing your hair, with the most delicate shampoo, and rinsing, and then drying your hair so gently with my soft towel, so that no murmur came from you, of discomfort or unease, and then looked into your eyes, and saw you look into mine, knowing that you wanted no one else, no one at all, knowing that you were entirely happy in my arms, I knew also, for example, that I was at the same time sitting by an indifferent fire, alone in winter, in eternal night without you.

VOICE 1

Lady Withers plays the piano. They were sitting, the three women, about the room. About the room were bottles of a vin rosé, of a pink I shall never forget. They sipped their wine from such lovely glass, an elegance of gesture and grace I thought long dead. Lady Withers wore a necklace around her alabaster neck, a neck amazingly young. She played Schumann. She smiled at me. Mrs Withers and Jane smiled at me. I took a seat. I took it and sat in it. I am in it. I will never leave it.

Oh mother, I have found my home, my family. Little did I ever dream I could know such happiness.

VOICE 2

Perhaps I should forget all about you. Perhaps I should curse you as your father cursed you. Oh I pray, I pray

141

your life is a torment to you. I wait for your letter
begging me to come to you. I'll spit on it.

VOICE 1
Mother, mother, I've had the most unpleasant, the most
mystifying encounter, with the man who calls himself
Mr Withers. Will you give me your advice?

Come in here, son, he called. Look sharp. Don't mess
about. I haven't got all night. I went in. A jug. A basin.
A bicycle.

You know where you are? he said. You're in my room.
It's not Euston Station. Get me? It's a true oasis.

This is the only room in this house where you can pick
up a caravanserai to all points West. Compris?
Comprende? Get me? Are you prepared to follow me
down the mountain? Look at me. My name's Withers.
I'm there or thereabouts. Follow? Embargo on all duff
terminology. With me? Embargo on all things
redundant. All areas in that connection verboten.
You're in a diseaseridden land, boxer. Keep your weight
on all the left feet you can lay your hands on. Keep
dancing. The old foxtrot is the classical response but
that's not the response I'm talking about. Nor am I
talking about the other response. Up the slaves. Get me?
This is a place of creatures, up and down stairs.
Creatures of the rhythmic splits, the rhythmic
sideswipes, the rums and roulettes, the macaroni tatters,
the dumplings in jam mayonnaise, a catapulting ordure
of gross and ramshackle shenanigans, openended

paraphernalia. Follow me? It all adds up. It's before you and behind you. I'm the only saviour of the grace you find yourself wanting in. Mind how you go. Look sharp. Get my drift? Don't let it get too mouldy. Watch the mould. Get the feel of it, sonny, get the density. Look at me.

And I did.

VOICE 2

I am ill.

VOICE 1

It was like looking into a pit of molten lava, mother. One look was enough for me.

VOICE 2

Come to me.

VOICE 1

I joined Mrs Withers for a Campari and soda in the kitchen. She spoke of her youth. I was a right titbit, she said. I was like a piece of plum duff. They used to come from miles to try their luck. I fell head over heels with a man in the Fleet Air Arm. He adored me. They had him murdered because they didn't want us to know happiness. I could have married him and had tons of sons. But oh no. He went down with his ship. I heard it on the wireless.

VOICE 2

I wait for you.

VOICE 1

Later that night Riley and I shared a cup of cocoa in his quarters. I like slender lads, Riley said. Slender but strong. I've never made any secret of it. But I've had to restrain myself, I've had to keep a tight rein on my inclinations. That's because my deepest disposition is towards religion. I've always been a deeply religious man. You can imagine the tension this creates in my soul. I walk about in a constant state of spiritual, emotional, psychological and physical tension. It's breathtaking, the discipline I'm called upon to exert. My lust is unimaginably violent but it goes against my best interests,which are to keep on the right side of God. I'm a big man, as you see, I could crush a slip of a lad such as you to death, I mean the death that is love, the death I understand love to be. But meet it is that I keep those desires shackled in handcuffs and leg-irons. I'm good at that sort of thing because I'm a policeman by trade. And I'm highly respected. I'm highly respected both in the force and in church. The only place where I'm not highly respected is in this house. They don't give a shit for me here. Although I've always been a close relation. Of a sort. I'm a fine tenor but they never invite me to sing. I might as well be living in the middle of the Sahara Desert. There are too many women here, that's the trouble. And it's no use talking to Baldy. He's well away. He lives in another area, best known to himself. I like health and strength and intelligent conversation. That's why I took a fancy to you, chum, apart from the fact that I fancy you. I've got no-one to talk to. These women treat me like a leper. Even though I am a relation. Of a sort.

What relation?

Is Lady Withers Jane's mother or sister?

If either is the case why isn't Jane called Lady Jane Withers? Or perhaps she is. Or perhaps neither is the case? Or perhaps Mrs Withers is actually the Honourable Mrs Withers? But if that is the case what does that make Mr Withers? And which Withers is he anyway? I mean what relation is he to the rest of the Witherses? And who is Riley?

But if you find me bewildered, anxious, confused, uncertain and afraid, you also find me content. My life possesses shape. The house has a very warm atmosphere, as you have no doubt gleaned. And as you have no doubt noted from my account I talk freely to all its inhabitants, with the exception of Mr Withers, to whom no one talks, to whom no one refers, with evidently good reason. But I rarely leave the house. No one seems to leave the house. Riley leaves the house but rarely. He must be a secret policeman. Jane continues to do a great deal of homework while not apparently attending any school. Lady Withers never leaves the house. She has guests. She receives guests. Those are the steps I hear on the stairs at night.

VOICE 3

I know your mother has written to you to tell you that I am dead. I am not dead. I am very far from being dead, although lots of people have wished me dead, from time immemorial, you especially. It is you who have prayed for my death, from time immemorial. I have heard your prayers. They ring in my ears. Prayers yearning for my death. But I am not dead.

Well, that is not entirely true, not entirely the case. I'm lying. I'm leading you up the garden path, I'm playing about, I'm having my bit of fun, that's what. Because I am dead. As dead as a doornail. I'm writing to you from my grave. A quick word for old time's sake. Just to keep in touch. An old hullo out of the dark. A last kiss from Dad.

I'll probably call it a day after this canter. Not much more to say. All a bit of a sweat. Why am I taking the trouble? Because of you, I suppose, because you were such a loving son. I'm smiling, as I lie in this glassy grave.

Do you know why I use the word glassy? Because I can see out of it.

Lots of love, son. Keep up the good work.

There's only one thing bothers me, to be quite frank. While there is, generally, absolute silence everywhere, absolute silence throughout all the hours, I still hear, occasionally, a dog barking. I hear this dog. Oh, it frightens me.

VOICE I

They have decided on a name for me. They call me Bobo. Good morning, Bobo, they say, or, See you in the morning, Bobo, or, Don't drop a goolie, Bobo, or, Don't forget the diver, Bobo, or, Keep your eye on the ball,

Bobo, or, Keep this side of the tramlines, Bobo, or,
How's the lead in your pencil, Bobo, or, How's tricks in
the sticks, Bobo, or, Don't get too much gum in your
gumboots, Bobo.

The only person who does not call me Bobo is the old
man. He calls me nothing. I call him nothing. I don't see
him. He keeps to his room. I don't go near it. He is old
and will die soon.

VOICE 2

The police are looking for you. You may remember that
you are still under twenty-one. They have issued your
precise description to all the organs. They will not rest,
they assure me, until you are found. I have stated my
belief that you are in the hands of underworld figures
who are using you as a male prostitute. I have declared
in my affidavit that you have never possessed any
strength of character whatsoever and that you are
palpably susceptible to even the most blatant form of
flattery and blandishment. Women were your downfall,
even as a nipper. I haven't forgotten Françoise the
French maid or the woman who masqueraded under the
title of governess, the infamous Miss Carmichael. You
will be found, my boy, and no mercy will be shown to
you.

VOICE 1

I'm coming back to you, mother, to hold you in my
arms.

I am coming home.

I am coming also to clasp my father's shoulder. Where is
the old boy? I'm longing to have a word with him.
Where is he? I've looked in all the usual places,
including the old summerhouse, but I can't find him.
Don't tell me he's left home at his age? That would be
inexpressibly skittish a gesture, on his part. What have
you done with him, mother?

VOICE 2
I'll tell you what, my darling. I've given you up as a
very bad job. Tell me one last thing. Do you think the
word love means anything?

VOICE 1
I am on my way back to you. I am about to make the
journey back to you. What will you say to me?

VOICE 3
I have so much to say to you. But I am quite dead.
What I have to say to you will never be said.

A KIND OF ALASKA

A Kind of Alaska was inspired by *Awakenings* by Oliver Sacks M.D., first published in 1973 by Gerald Duckworth and Co.

In the winter of 1916–17, there spread over Europe, and subsequently over the rest of the world, an extraordinary epidemic illness which presented itself in innumerable forms – as delirium, mania, trances, coma, sleep, insomnia, restlessness, and states of Parkinsonism. It was eventually identified by the great physician Constantin von Economo and named by him *encephalitis lethargica*, or sleeping sickness.

Over the next ten years almost five million people fell victim to the disease of whom more than a third died. Of the survivors some escaped almost unscathed, but the majority moved into states of deepening illness. The worst affected sank into singular states of 'sleep' – conscious of their surroundings but motionless, speechless, and without hope or will, confined to asylums or other institutions.

Fifty years later, with the development of the remarkable drug L-DOPA, they erupted into life once more.

A Kind of Alaska was presented with *Victoria Station* and *Family Voices* as part of the triple bill, *Other Places*, first performed at the National Theatre, London, on 14 October 1982 with the following cast:

DEBORAH	Judi Dench
HORNBY	Paul Rogers
PAULINE	Anna Massey

Directed by Peter Hall

It was subsequently presented with *Victoria Station* and *One for the Road* at the Duchess Theatre, London, on 7 March 1985 with the following cast:

DEBORAH	Dorothy Tutin
HORNBY	Colin Blakely
PAULINE	Susan Engel

Directed by Kenneth Ives

It was produced by Central Television in December 1984 with the following cast:

DEBORAH	Dorothy Tutin
HORNBY	Paul Scofield
PAULINE	Susan Engel

Directed by Kenneth Ives

A woman in a white bed. Mid-forties. She sits up against high-banked pillows, stares ahead.

A table and two chairs. A window.

A man in a dark suit sits at the table. Early sixties.

The woman's eyes move. She slowly looks about her.

Her gaze passes over the man and on.
He watches her.

She stares ahead, still.

She whispers.

DEBORAH

Something is happening.

Silence.

HORNBY

Do you know me?

Silence.

Do you recognise me?

153

Silence.

Can you hear me?

She does not look at him.

DEBORAH

Are you speaking?

HORNBY

Yes.

Pause.

Do you know who I am?

Pause.

Who am I?

DEBORAH

No one hears what I say. No one is listening to me.

Pause.

HORNBY

Do you know who I am?

Pause.

Who am I?

DEBORAH

You are no-one.

Pause.

Who is it? It is miles away. The rain is falling. I will get wet.

Pause.

I can't get to sleep. The dog keeps turning about. I think he's dreaming. He wakes me up, but not himself up. He's my best dog though. I talk French.

Pause.

HORNBY

I would like you to listen to me.

Pause.

You have been asleep for a very long time. You have now woken up. We are here to care for you.

Pause.

You have been asleep for a very long time. You are older, although you do not know that. You are still young, but older.

Pause.

DEBORAH

Something is happening.

HORNBY

You have been asleep. You have awoken. Can you hear me? Do you understand me?

She looks at him for the first time.

DEBORAH

Asleep?

Pause.

I do not remember that.

Pause.

People have been looking at me. They have been touching me. I spoke, but I don't think they heard what I said.

Pause.

What language am I speaking? I speak French, I know that. Is this French?

Pause.

I've not seen Daddy today. He's funny. He makes me laugh. He runs with me. We play with balloons.

Pause.

Where is he?

Pause.

I think it's my birthday soon.

Pause.

No, no. No, no. I sleep like other people. No more no less. Why should I? If I sleep late my mother wakes me up. There are things to do.

Pause.

If I have been asleep, why hasn't Mummy woken me up?

HORNBY

I have woken you up.

DEBORAH

But I don't know you.

Pause.

Where is everyone? Where is my dog? Where are my sisters? Last night Estelle was wearing my dress. But I said she could.

Pause.

I am cold.

HORNBY

How old are you?

DEBORAH

I am twelve. No. I am sixteen. I am seven.

Pause.

I don't know. Yes. I know. I am fourteen. I am fifteen.
I'm lovely fifteen.

Pause.

You shouldn't have brought me here. My mother will
ask me where I've been.

Pause.

You shouldn't have touched me like that. I shan't tell
my mother. I shouldn't have touched you like that.

Pause.

Oh Jack.

Pause.

It's time I was up and about. All those dogs are making
such a racket. I suppose Daddy's feeding them. Is Estelle
going to marry that boy from Townley Street? The ginger
boy? Pauline says he's got nothing between his ears.
Thick as two planks. I've given it a good deal of rather
more mature thought and I've decided she should not

marry him. Tell her not to marry him. She'll listen to you.

Pause.

Daddy?

HORNBY

She didn't marry him.

DEBORAH

Didn't?

Pause.

It would be a great mistake. It would ruin her life.

HORNBY

She didn't marry him.

Silence.

DEBORAH

I've seen this room before. What room is this? It's not my bedroom. My bedroom has blue lilac on the walls. The sheets are soft, pretty. Mummy kisses me.

Pause.

This is not my bedroom.

HORNBY

You have been in this room for a long time. You have been asleep. You have now woken up.

159

DEBORAH

You shouldn't have brought me here. What are you saying? Did I ask you to bring me here? Did I make eyes at you? Did I show desire for you? Did I let you peep up my skirt? Did I flash my teeth? Was I as bold as brass? Perhaps I've forgotten.

HORNBY

I didn't bring you here. Your mother and father brought you here.

DEBORAH

My father? My mother?

Pause.

Did they bring me to you as a sacrifice? Did they sacrifice me to you?

Pause.

No, no. You stole me . . . in the night.

Pause.

Have you had your way with me?

HORNBY

I am here to take care of you.

DEBORAH

They all say that.

Pause.

You've had your way with me. You made me touch
you. You stripped me. I cried . . . but . . . but it was my
lust made me cry. You are a devil. My lust was my own.
I kept it by me. You took it from me. Once open never
closed. Never closed again. Never closed always open.
For eternity. Terrible. You have ruined me.

Pause.

I sound childish. Out of . . . tune.

Pause.

How old am I?

Pause.

Eighteen?

HORNBY

No.

DEBORAH

Well then, I've no idea how old I am. Do you know?

HORNBY

Not exactly.

DEBORAH

Why not?

Pause.

My sisters would know. We're very close. We love each other. We're known as the three bluebells.

Pause.

Why is everything so quiet? So still? I'm in a sandbag. The sea. Is that what I hear? A long way away. Gulls. Haven't heard a gull for ages. God what a racket. Where's Pauline? She's such a mischief. I have to keep telling her not to be so witty. That's what I say. You're too witty for your own good. You're so sharp you'll cut yourself. You're too witty for your own tongue. You'll bite your own tongue off one of these days and I'll keep your tongue in a closed jar and you'll never ever ever ever be witty again.

Pause.

She's all right, really. She just talks too much. Whereas Estelle is as deep as a pond. She's marvellous at crossing her legs. Sen-su-al.

Pause.

This is a hotel. A hotel near the sea. Hastings? Torquay? There's more to this than meets the eye. I'm coming to that conclusion. There's something very shady about you. Pauline always says I'll end up as part of the White Slave Traffic.

Pause.

Yes. This is a white tent. When I open the flap I'll step out into the Sahara Desert.

HORNBY

You've been asleep.

DEBORAH

Oh, you keep saying that! What's wrong with that? Why shouldn't I have a long sleep for a change? I need it. My body demands it. It's quite natural. I may have overslept but I didn't do it deliberately. If I had any choice in the matter I'd much prefer to be up and about. I love the morning. Why do you blame me? I was simply obeying the law of the body.

HORNBY

I know that. I'm not blaming you.

DEBORAH

Well, how long have I been asleep?

Pause.

HORNBY

You have been asleep for twenty-nine years.

Silence.

DEBORAH

You mean I'm dead?

HORNBY

No.

DEBORAH

I don't feel dead.

HORNBY

You're not.

DEBORAH

But you mean I've been dead?

HORNBY

If you had been dead you wouldn't be alive now.

DEBORAH

Are you sure?

HORNBY

No one wakes from the dead.

DEBORAH

No, I shouldn't think so.

Pause.

Well, what was I doing if I wasn't dead?

HORNBY

We don't know . . . what you were doing.

DEBORAH

We?

Pause.

Where's my mother? My father? Estelle? Pauline?

HORNBY

Pauline is here. She's waiting to see you.

DEBORAH

She shouldn't be out at this time of night. I'm always
telling her. She needs her beauty sleep. Like I do, by the
way. But of course I'm her elder sister so she doesn't
listen to me. And Estelle doesn't listen to me because
she's my elder sister. That's family life. And Jack?
Where's Jack? Where's my boyfriend? He's my
boyfriend. He loves me. He loves me. I once saw him
cry. For love. Don't make him cry again. What have you
done to him? What have you done with him? What?
What? What?

HORNBY

Be calm. Don't agitate yourself.

DEBORAH

Agitate myself?

HORNBY

There's no hurry about any of this.

DEBORAH

Any of what?

HORNBY

Be calm.

DEBORAH

I am calm.

Pause.

I've obviously committed a criminal offence and am now in prison. I'm quite prepared to face up to the facts. But what offence? I can't imagine what offence it could be. I mean one that would bring . . . such a terrible sentence.

HORNBY

This is not a prison. You have committed no offence.

DEBORAH

But what have I done? What have I been doing? Where have I been?

HORNBY

Do you remember nothing of where you've been? Do you remember nothing . . . of all that has happened to you?

DEBORAH

Nothing has happened to me. I've been nowhere.

Silence.

HORNBY

I think we should –

DEBORAH

I certainly don't want to see Pauline. People don't want

to see their sisters. They're only their sisters. They're so witty. All I hear is chump chump. The side teeth. Eating everything in sight. Gold chocolate. So greedy eat it with the paper on. Munch all the ratshit on the sideboard. Someone has to polish it off. Been there for years. Statues of excrement. Wrapped in gold. I've never got used to it. Sisters are diabolical. Brothers are worse. One day I prayed I would see no one ever again, none of them ever again. All that eating, all that wit.

Pause.

HORNBY

I didn't know you had any brothers.

DEBORAH

What?

Pause.

HORNBY

Come. Rest. Tomorrow . . . is another day.

DEBORAH

No it isn't. No it isn't. It is not!

She smiles.

Yes, of course it is. Of course it is. Tomorrow is another day. I'd love to ask you a question.

HORNBY

Are you not tired?

DEBORAH

Tired? Not at all. I'm wide awake. Don't you think so?

HORNBY

What is the question?

DEBORAH

How did you wake me up?

Pause.

Or did you not wake me up? Did I just wake up myself? All by myself? Or did you wake me with a magic wand?

HORNBY

I woke you with an injection.

DEBORAH

Lovely injection. Oh how I love it. And am I beautiful?

HORNBY

Certainly.

DEBORAH

And you are my Prince Charming. Aren't you?

Pause.

Oh speak up.

Pause.

Silly shit. All men are alike.

Pause.

I think I love you.

HORNBY

No, you don't.

DEBORAH

Well, I'm not spoilt for choice here, am I? There's not
another man in sight. What have you done with all the
others? There's a boy called Peter. We play with his
trains, we play . . . Cowboys and Indians . . . I'm a
tomboy. I knock him about. But that was . . .

Pause.

But now I've got all the world before me. All life before
me. All my life before me.

Pause.

I've had enough of this. Find Jack. I'll say yes. We'll
have kids. I'll bake apples. I'm ready for it. No point in
hanging about. Best foot forward. Mummy's motto. Bit
of a cheek, I think, Mummy not coming in to say
hullo, to say good night, to tuck me up, to sing me a
song, to warn me about going too far with boys.
Daddy I love but he is a bit absent-minded. Thinking
of other things. That's what Pauline says. She says he
has a mistress in Fulham. The bitch. I mean Pauline.
And she's only . . . thirteen. I keep telling her I'm not
prepared to tolerate her risible, her tendentious, her
eclectic, her ornate, her rococo insinuations and

garbled inventions. I tell her that every day of the
week.

Pause.

Daddy is kind and so is Mummy. We all have breakfast
together every morning in the kitchen. What's
happening?

Pause.

HORNBY

One day suddenly you stopped.

DEBORAH

Stopped?

HORNBY

Yes.

Pause.

You fell asleep and no one could wake you. But
although I use the word sleep, it was not strictly sleep.

DEBORAH

Oh, make up your mind!

Pause.

You mean you thought I was asleep but I was actually
awake?

HORNBY

Neither asleep nor awake.

DEBORAH

Was I dreaming?

HORNBY

Were you?

DEBORAH

Well was I? I don't know.

Pause.

I'm not terribly pleased about all this. I'm going to ask a few questions in a few minutes. One of them might be: What did I look like while I was asleep, or while I was awake, or whatever it was I was? Bet you can't tell me.

HORNBY

You were quite still. Fixed. Most of the time.

DEBORAH

Show me.

Pause.

Show me what I looked like.

He demonstrates a still, fixed position.
She studies him. She laughs, stops abruptly.

Most of the time? What about the rest of the time?

HORNBY

You were taken for walks twice a week. We encouraged your legs to move.

Pause.

At other times you would suddenly move of your own volition very quickly, very quickly indeed, spasmodically, for short periods, and as suddenly as you began you would stop.

Pause.

DEBORAH

Did you ever see . . . tears . . . well in my eyes?

HORNBY

No.

DEBORAH

And when I laughed . . . did you laugh with me?

HORNBY

You never laughed.

DEBORAH

Of course I laughed. I have a laughing nature.

Pause.

Right. I'll get up now.

He moves to her.

No! Don't! Don't be ridiculous.

She eases herself out of the bed, stands, falls. He moves to her.

No! Don't! Don't! Don't! Don't touch me.

She stands, very slowly. He retreats, watching.
She stands still, begins to walk, in slow motion, towards him.

Let us dance.

She dances, by herself, in slow motion.

I dance.

She dances.

I've kept in practice, you know. I've been dancing in very narrow spaces. Kept stubbing my toes and bumping my head. Like Alice. Shall I sit here? I shall sit here.

She sits at the table. He joins her.
She touches the arms of her chair, touches the table, examines the table.

I like tables, don't you? This is a rather beautiful table. Any chance of a dry sherry?

HORNBY
Not yet. Soon we'll have a party for you.

DEBORAH

A party? For me? How nice. Lots of cakes and lots of booze?

HORNBY

That's right.

DEBORAH

How nice.

Pause.

Well, it's nice at this table. What's the news? I suppose the war's still over?

HORNBY

It's over, yes.

DEBORAH

Oh good. They haven't started another one?

HORNBY

No.

DEBORAH

Oh good.

Pause.

HORNBY

You danced in narrow spaces?

DEBORAH

Oh yes. The most crushing spaces. The most punishing spaces. That was tough going. Very difficult. Like dancing with someone dancing on your foot all the time, I mean *all* the time, on the same spot, just slam, slam, a big boot on your foot, not the most ideal kind of dancing, not by a long chalk. But sometimes the space opened and became light, sometimes it opened and I was so light, and when you feel so light you can dance till dawn and I danced till dawn night after night, night after night . . . for a time . . . I think . . . until . . .

She has become aware of the figure of PAULINE, *standing in the room. She stares at her.*
PAULINE *is a woman in her early forties.*

PAULINE

Deborah.

DEBORAH *stares at her.*

Deborah. It's Pauline.

PAULINE *turns to* HORNBY.

She's looking at me.

She turns back to DEBORAH.

You're looking at me. Oh Deborah . . . you haven't looked at me . . . for such a long time.

Pause.

I'm your sister. Do you know me?

DEBORAH *laughs shortly and turns away.*
HORNBY *stands and goes to* PAULINE.

HORNBY

I didn't call you.

PAULINE *regards him.*

Well, all right. Speak to her.

PAULINE

What shall I say?

HORNBY

Just talk to her.

PAULINE

Doesn't it matter what I say?

HORNBY

No.

PAULINE

I can't do her harm?

HORNBY

No.

PAULINE

Shall I tell her lies or the truth?

HORNBY

Both.

Pause.

PAULINE

You're trembling.

HORNBY

Am I?

PAULINE

Your hand.

HORNBY

Is it?

He looks at his hand.

Trembling? Is it? Yes.

PAULINE *goes to* DEBORAH, *sits with her at the table.*

PAULINE

Debby. I've spoken to the family. Everyone was so
happy. I spoke to them all, in turn. They're away, you
see. They're on a world cruise. They deserve it. It's been
so hard for them. And Daddy's not too well, although
in many respects he's as fit as a fiddle, and Mummy . . .
It's a wonderful trip. They passed through the Indian
Ocean. And the Bay of Bosphorus. Can you imagine?
Estelle also . . . needed a total break. It's a wonderful
trip. Quite honestly, it's the trip of a lifetime. They've

stopped off in Bangkok. That's where I found them. I spoke to them all, in turn. And they all send so much love to you. Especially Mummy.

Pause.

I spoke by radio telephone. Shore to ship. The captain's cabin. Such excitement.

Pause.

Tell me. Do you . . . remember me?

DEBORAH *stands and walks to her bed, in slow motion.*
Very slowly she gets into the bed.
She lies against the pillow, closes her eyes.
She opens her eyes, looks at PAULINE, *beckons to her.*
PAULINE *goes to the bed.*

DEBORAH
Let me look into your eyes.

She looks deeply into PAULINE*'s eyes.*

So you say you're my sister?

PAULINE
I am.

DEBORAH
Well, you've changed. A great deal. You've aged . . . substantially. What happened to you?

DEBORAH *turns to* HORNBY.

What happened to her? Was it a sudden shock? I know shocks can age people overnight. Someone told me.

She turns to PAULINE.

Is that what happened to you? Did a sudden shock age you overnight?

PAULINE
No it was you –

PAULINE *looks at* HORNBY. *He looks back at her, impassive.* PAULINE *turns back to* DEBORAH.

It was you. You were standing with a vase of flowers in your hands. You were about to put it down on the table. But you didn't put it down. You stood still, with the vase in your hands, as if you were . . . fixed. I was with you, in the room. I looked into your eyes.

Pause.

I said: 'Debby?'

Pause.

But you remained . . . quite . . . still. I touched you. I said: 'Debby?' Your eyes were open. You were looking nowhere. Then you suddenly looked at me and saw me and smiled at me and put the vase down on the table.

Pause.

But at the end of dinner, we were all laughing and
talking, and Daddy was making jokes and making us
laugh, and you said you couldn't see him properly
because of the flowers in the middle of the table, where
you had put them, and you stood and picked up the
vase and you took it towards that little sidetable by the
window, walnut, and Mummy was laughing and even
Estelle was laughing and then we suddenly looked at
you and you had stopped. You were standing with the
vase by the sidetable, you were about to put it down,
your arm was stretched towards it but you had
stopped.

Pause.

We went to you. We spoke to you. Mummy touched
you. She spoke to you.

Pause.

Then Daddy tried to take the vase from you. He could
not . . . wrench it from your hands. He could not . . .
move you from the spot. Like . . . marble.

Pause.

You were sixteen.

DEBORAH *turns to* HORNBY.

DEBORAH

She must be an aunt I never met. One of those distant cousins.

(*To* PAULINE:) Have you left me money in your Will? Well, I could do with it.

PAULINE

I'm Pauline.

DEBORAH

Well, if you're Pauline you've put on a remarkable amount of weight in a very short space of time. I can see you're not keeping up with your ballet classes. My God! You've grown breasts!

DEBORAH *stares at* PAULINE's *breasts and suddenly looks down at herself.*

PAULINE

We're women.

DEBORAH

Women?

HORNBY

You're a grown woman, Deborah.

DEBORAH (*to* PAULINE:)

Is Estelle going to marry that ginger boy from Townley Street?

HORNBY

Deborah. Listen. You're not listening.

DEBORAH

To what?

HORNBY

To what your sister has been saying.

DEBORAH (*to* PAULINE:)

Are you my sister?

PAULINE

Yes. Yes.

DEBORAH

But where did you get those breasts?

PAULINE

They came about.

DEBORAH *looks down at herself.*

DEBORAH

I'm slimmer. Aren't I?

PAULINE

Yes.

DEBORAH

Yes. I'm slimmer.

Pause.

I'm going to run into the sea and fall into the waves. I'm going to rummage about in all the water.

Pause.

Are we going out to dinner tonight?

Pause.

Where's Jack? Tongue-tied as usual. He's too shy for his own good. and Pauline's so sharp she'll cut herself. And Estelle's such a flibbertigibbet. I think she should marry that ginger boy from Townley Street and settle down before it's too late.

Pause.

PAULINE

I am a widow.

DEBORAH

This woman is mad.

HORNBY

No. She's not.

Pause.

She has been coming to see you regularly . . . for a long time. She has suffered for you. She has never forsaken you. Nor have I.

Pause.

I have been your doctor for many years. This is your
sister. Your father is blind. Estelle looks after him. She
never married. Your mother is dead.

Pause.

It was I who took the vase from your hands. I lifted you
onto this bed, like a corpse. Some wanted to bury you. I
forbade it. I have nourished you, watched over you, for
all this time.

Pause.

I injected you and woke you up. You will ask why I did
not inject you twenty-nine years ago. I'll tell you. I did
not possess the appropriate fluid.

Pause.

You see, you have been nowhere, absent, indifferent. It
is we who have suffered.

Pause.

You do see that, I'm sure. You were an extremely
intelligent young girl. All opinions confirm this. Your
mind has not been damaged. It was merely suspended,
it took up a temporary habitation . . . in a kind of
Alaska. But it was not entirely static, was it? You
ventured into quite remote . . . utterly foreign . . .
territories. You kept on the move. And I charted your
itinerary. Or did my best to do so. I have never let you
go.

184

Silence.

I have never let you go.

Silence.

I have lived with you.

Pause.

Your sister Pauline was twelve when you were left for dead. When she was twenty I married her. She is a widow. I have lived with you.

Silence.

                    DEBORAH
I want to go home.

Pause.

I'm cold.

She takes PAULINE's *hand.*

Is it my birthday soon? Will I have a birthday party? Will everyone be there? Will they all come? All our friends? How old will I be?

                    PAULINE
You will. You will have a birthday party. And everyone will be there. All your family will be there. All your old friends. And we'll have presents for you. All wrapped

up . . . wrapped up in such beautiful paper.

DEBORAH

What presents?

PAULINE

Ah, we're not going to tell you. We're not going to tell you that. Because they're a secret.

Pause.

Think of it. Think of the thrill . . . of opening them, of unwrapping them, of taking out your presents and looking at them.

DEBORAH

Can I keep them?

PAULINE

Of course you can keep them. They're your presents. They're for you . . . only.

DEBORAH

I might lose them.

PAULINE

No, no. We'll put them all around you in your bedroom. We'll see that nobody else touches them. Nobody will touch them. And we'll kiss you good night. And when you wake up in the morning your presents . . .

Pause.

———

DEBORAH

I don't want to lose them.

PAULINE

They'll never be lost. Ever.

Pause.

And we'll sing to you. What will we sing?

DEBORAH

What?

PAULINE

We'll sing 'Happy Birthday' to you.

Pause.

DEBORAH

Now what was I going to say?

She begins to flick her cheek, as if brushing something from it.

Now what –? Oh dear, oh no. Oh dear.

Pause.

Oh dear.

The flicking of her cheek grows faster.

Yes, I think they're closing in. They're closing in.
They're closing the walls in. Yes.

*She bows her head, flicking faster, her fingers now
moving about over her face.*

Oh . . . well . . . oooohhhhh . . . oh no . . . oh no . . .

*During the course of this speech her body becomes
hunchbacked.*

Let me out. Stop it. Let me out. Stop it. Stop it. Stop it.
Shutting the walls on me. Shutting them down on me.
So tight, so tight. Something panting, something
panting. Can't see. Oh, the light is going. The light is
going. They're shutting up shop. They're closing my
face. Chains and padlocks. Bolting me up. Stinking. The
smell. Oh my goodness, oh dear, oh my goodness, oh
dear, I'm so young. It's a vice. I'm in a vice. It's at the
back of my neck. Ah. Eyes stuck. Only see the shadow
of the tip of my nose. Shadow of the tip of my nose.
Eyes stuck.

*She stops flicking abruptly, sits still. Her body
straightens. She looks up. She looks at her fingers,
examines them.*

Nothing.

Silence.
She speaks calmly, is quite still.

Do you hear a drip?

Pause.

I hear a drip. Someone's left the tap on.

Pause.

I'll tell you what it is. It's a vast series of halls. With
enormous interior windows masquerading as walls. The
windows are mirrors, you see. And so glass reflects
glass. For ever and ever.

Pause.

You can't imagine how still it is. So silent I hear my eyes
move.

Silence.

I'm lying in bed. People bend over me, speak to me. I
want to say hullo, to have a chat, to make some
inquiries. But you can't do that if you're in a vast hall of
glass with a tap dripping.

Silence.
She looks at PAULINE.

I must be quite old. I wonder what I look like. But it's of
no consequence. I certainly have no intention of looking
into a mirror.

Pause.

No.

She looks at HORNBY.

You say I have been asleep. You say I am now awake.
You say I have not awoken from the dead. You say I
was not dreaming then and am not dreaming now. You
say I have always been alive and am alive now. You say
I am a woman.

She looks at PAULINE, *then back at* HORNBY.

She is a widow. She doesn't go to her ballet classes any
more. Mummy and Daddy and Estelle are on a world
cruise. They've stopped off in Bangkok. It'll be my
birthday soon. I think I have the matter in proportion.

Pause.

Thank you.

VICTORIA STATION

Victoria Station was presented as part of a triple bill, *Other Places*, first performed at the National Theatre, London, on 14 October 1982 with the following cast:

CONTROLLER   Paul Rogers
DRIVER   Martin Jarvis

Directed by Peter Hall

It was subsequently presented with *A Kind of Alaska* and *One for the Road* at the Duchess Theatre, London, on 7 March 1985 with the following cast:

CONTROLLER   Colin Blakely
DRIVER   Roger Davidson

Directed by Kenneth Ives

Lights up on office. CONTROLLER *sitting at microphone.*

CONTROLLER

274? Where are you?

Lights up on DRIVER *in car.*

CONTROLLER

274? Where are you?

Pause.

DRIVER

Hullo?

CONTROLLER

274?

DRIVER

Hullo?

CONTROLLER

Is that 274?

DRIVER

That's me.

193

CONTROLLER

Where are you?

DRIVER

What?

Pause.

CONTROLLER

I'm talking to 274? Right?

DRIVER

Yes. That's me. I'm 274. Who are you?

Pause.

CONTROLLER

Who am I?

DRIVER

Yes.

CONTROLLER

Who do you think I am? I'm your office.

DRIVER

Oh yes.

CONTROLLER

Where are you?

DRIVER

I'm cruising.

CONTROLLER

What do you mean?

Pause.

Listen son. I've got a job for you. If you're in the area I
think you're in. Where are you?

DRIVER

I'm just cruising about.

CONTROLLER

Don't cruise. Stop cruising. Nobody's asking you to
cruise about. What the fuck are you cruising about for?

Pause.

274?

DRIVER

Hullo. Yes. That's me.

CONTROLLER

I want you to go to Victoria Station. I want you to pick
up a customer coming from Boulogne. That is what I
want you to do. Do you follow me? Now the question I
want to ask you is this. Where are you? And don't say
you're just cruising about. Just tell me if you're
anywhere near Victoria Station.

DRIVER

Victoria what?

Pause.

CONTROLLER

Station.

Pause.

Can you help me on this?

DRIVER

Sorry?

CONTROLLER

Can you help me on this? Can you come to my aid on this?

Pause.

You see, 274, I've got no one else in the area, you see. I've only got you in the area. I think. Do you follow me?

DRIVER

I follow you, yes.

CONTROLLER

And this is a good job, 274. He wants you to take him to Cuckfield.

DRIVER

Eh?

CONTROLLER

He wants you to take him to Cuckfield. You're meeting the 10.22 from Boulogne. The European Special. His name's MacRooney. He's a little bloke with a limp. I've known him for years. You pick him up under the clock. You'll know him by his hat. He'll have a hat on with a feather in it. He'll be carrying fishing tackle. 274?

DRIVER

Hullo?

CONTROLLER

Are you hearing me?

DRIVER

Yes.

Pause.

CONTROLLER

What are you doing?

DRIVER

I'm not doing anything.

CONTROLLER

How's your motor? Is your motor working?

DRIVER

Oh yes.

CONTROLLER

Your ignition's not on the blink?

CONTROLLER

No.

CONTROLLER

So you're sitting in a capable car?

DRIVER

I'm sitting in it, yes.

CONTROLLER

Are you in the driving seat?

Pause.

Do you understand what I mean?

Pause.

Do you have a driving wheel in front of you?

Pause.

Because I haven't, 274. I'm just talking into this machine, trying to make some sense out of our lives. That's my function. God gave me this job. He asked me to do this job, personally. I'm your local monk, 274. I'm a monk. You follow? I lead a restricted life. I haven't got a choke and a gear lever in front of me. I haven't got a cooling system and four wheels. I'm not sitting here with wing mirrors and a jack in the boot. And if I did have a jack in the boot I'd stick it right up your arse.

Pause.

Listen, 274. I've got every reason to believe that you're driving a Ford Cortina. I would very much like you to go to Victoria Station. *In* it. That means I don't want you to walk down there. I want you to drive down there. Right?

DRIVER

Everything you say is correct. This is a Ford Cortina.

CONTROLLER

Good. That's right. And you're sitting in it while we're having this conversation, aren't you?

DRIVER

That's right.

CONTROLLER

Where?

DRIVER

By the side of a park.

CONTROLLER

By the side of a park?

DRIVER

Yes.

CONTROLLER

What park?

DRIVER

A dark park.

CONTROLLER

Why is it dark?

Pause.

DRIVER

That's not an easy question.

Pause.

CONTROLLER

Isn't it?

DRIVER

No.

Pause.

CONTROLLER

You remember this customer I was talking to you about? The one who's coming in to Victoria Station? Well, he's very keen for you to take him down to Cuckfield. He's got an old aunt down there. I've got a funny feeling she's going to leave him all her plunder. He's going down to pay his respects. He'll be in a good mood. If you play your cards right you might come out in front. Get me?

Pause.

274?

                    DRIVER
Yes? I'm here.

                    CONTROLLER
Go to Victoria Station.

                    DRIVER
I don't know it.

                    CONTROLLER
You don't know it?

                    DRIVER
No. What is it?

Silence.

                    CONTROLLER
It's a station, 274.

Pause.

Haven't you heard of it?

                    DRIVER
No. Never. What kind of place is it?

Pause.

                    CONTROLLER
You've never heard of Victoria Station?

DRIVER
Never. No.

CONTROLLER
It's a famous station.

DRIVER
Well, I honestly don't know what I've been doing all these years.

CONTROLLER
What have you been doing all these years?

DRIVER
Well, I honestly don't know.

Pause.

CONTROLLER
All right 274. Report to the office in the morning. 135? Where are you? 135? Where are you?

DRIVER
Don't leave me.

CONTROLLER
What? Who's that?

DRIVER
It's me. 274. Please. Don't leave me.

CONTROLLER
135? Where are you?

DRIVER

Don't have anything to do with 135. He's not your
man. He'll lead you into blind alleys by the dozen. They
all will. Don't leave me. I'm your man. I'm the only one
you can trust.

Pause.

CONTROLLER

Do I know you, 274? Have we met?

Pause.

Well, it'll be nice to meet you in the morning. I'm really
looking forward to it. I'll be sitting here with my cat
o'nine tails, son. And you know what I'm going to do
with it? I'm going to tie you up bollock naked to a
butcher's table and I'm going to flog you to death all the
way to Crystal Palace.

DRIVER

That's where I am! I knew I knew the place.

Pause.

I'm sitting by a little dark park underneath Crystal
Palace. I can see the Palace. It's silhouetted against the
sky. It's a wonderful edifice, isn't it?

Pause.

My wife's in bed. Probably asleep. And I've got a little
daughter.

CONTROLLER

Oh, you've got a little daughter?

Pause.

DRIVER

Yes, I think that's what she is.

CONTROLLER

Report to the office at 9 a.m. 135? Where are you? Where the fuck is 135? 246? 178? 101? Will somebody help me? Where's everyone gone? I've got a good job going down to Cuckfield. Can anyone hear me?

DRIVER

I can hear you.

CONTROLLER

Who's that?

DRIVER

274. Here. Waiting. What do you want me to do?

CONTROLLER

You want to know what I want you to do?

DRIVER

Oh by the way, there's something I forgot to tell you.

CONTROLLER

What is it?

DRIVER

I've got a P.O.B.

CONTROLLER

You've got a P.O.B.?

DRIVER

Yes. That means passenger on board.

CONTROLLER

I know what it means, 274. It means you've got a
passenger on board.

DRIVER

That's right.

CONTROLLER

You've got a passenger on board sitting by the side of a
park?

DRIVER

That's right.

CONTROLLER

Did I book this job?

DRIVER

No, I don't think you came into it.

CONTROLLER

Well, where does he want to go?

DRIVER

He doesn't want to go anywhere. We just cruised about
for a bit and then we came to rest.

CONTROLLER

In Crystal Palace?

DRIVER

Not *in* the Palace.

CONTROLLER

Oh, you're not *in* the Palace?

DRIVER

No. I'm not right inside it.

CONTROLLER

I think you'll find the Crystal Palace burnt down years
ago, old son. It burnt down in the Great Fire of
London.

Pause.

DRIVER

Did it?

CONTROLLER

274?

DRIVER

Yes. I'm here.

CONTROLLER

Drop your passenger. Drop your passenger at his
chosen destination and proceed to Victoria Station.
Otherwise I'll destroy you bone by bone. I'll suck you in
and blow you out in little bubbles. I'll chew your
stomach out with my own teeth. I'll eat all the hair off
your body. You'll end up looking like a pipe cleaner.
Get me?

Pause.

274?

Pause.

You're beginning to obsess me. I think I'm going to die.
I'm alone in this miserable freezing fucking office and
nobody loves me. Listen, pukeface –

DRIVER

Yes?

Pause.

CONTROLLER

135? 135? Where are you?

DRIVER

Don't have anything to do with 135. They're all
bloodsuckers. I'm the only one you can trust.

Pause.

CONTROLLER

You know what I've always dreamed of doing? I've always had this dream of having a holiday in sunny Barbados. I'm thinking of taking this holiday at the end of this year, 274. I'd like you to come with me. To Barbados. Just the two of us. I'll take you snorkelling. We can swim together in the blue Caribbean.

Pause.

In the meantime, though, why don't you just pop back to the office now and I'll make you a nice cup of tea? You can tell me something about your background, about your ambitions and aspirations. You can tell me all about your little hobbies and pastimes. Come over and have a nice cup of tea, 274.

DRIVER

I'd love to but I've got a passenger on board.

CONTROLLER

Put your passenger on to me. Let me have a word with him.

DRIVER

I can't. She's asleep on the back seat.

CONTROLLER

She?

DRIVER

Can I tell you a secret?

CONTROLLER

Please do.

DRIVER

I think I've fallen in love. For the first time in my life.

CONTROLLER

Who have you fallen in love with?

DRIVER

With this girl on the back seat. I think I'm going to keep
her for the rest of my life. I'm going to stay in this car
with her for the rest of my life. I'm going to marry her
in this car. We'll die together in this car.

Pause.

CONTROLLER

So you've found true love at last, eh, 274?

DRIVER

Yes. I've found true love at last.

CONTROLLER

So you're a happy man now then, are you?

DRIVER

I'm very happy. I've never known such happiness.

CONTROLLER

Well, I'd like to be the first to congratulate you, 274. I'd
like to extend my sincere felicitations to you.

DRIVER

Thank you very much.

CONTROLLER

Don't mention it. I'll have to make a note in my diary
not to forget your Golden Wedding, won't I? I'll bring
along some of the boys to drink your health. Yes, I'll
bring along some of the boys. We'll all have a few jars
and a bit of a sing-song.

Pause.

274?

Pause.

DRIVER

Hullo. Yes. It's me.

CONTROLLER

Listen. I've been thinking. I've decided that what I'd like
to do now is to come down there and shake you by the
hand straightaway. I'm going to shut this little office
and I'm going to jump into my old car and I'm going to
pop down to see you, to shake you by the hand. All
right?

DRIVER

Fine. But what about this man coming off the train at
Victoria Station – the 10.22 from Boulogne?

CONTROLLER

He can go and fuck himself.

DRIVER

I see.

CONTROLLER

No, I'd like to meet your lady friend, you see. And we can have a nice celebration. Can't we? So just stay where you are. Right?

Pause.

Right?

Pause.

274?

DRIVER

Yes?

CONTROLLER

Don't move. Stay exactly where you are. I'll be right with you.

DRIVER

No, I won't move.

Silence.

I'll be here.

Light out in office.
The DRIVER sits still.
Light out in car.

PRECISELY

Precisely was first performed in *The Big One* at the Apollo Theatre, London, on 18 December 1983. The cast was as follows:

STEPHEN   Barry Foster
ROGER   Martin Jarvis

Directed by Harold Pinter

Two men at a table with drinks.

Silence.

STEPHEN
I mean, we've said it time and time again, haven't we?

ROGER
Of course we have.

STEPHEN
Time and time again. Twenty million. That's what we've
said. Time and time again. It's a figure supported by
facts. We've done our homework. Twenty million is a
fact. When these people say thirty I'll tell you exactly
what they're doing – they're distorting the facts.

ROGER
Scandalous.

STEPHEN
Quite. I mean, how the hell do they *know*?

ROGER
Quite.

STEPHEN

We've done the *thinking*.

ROGER

Quite.

STEPHEN

That's what we're paid for.

ROGER

Paid a bloody lot too.

STEPHEN

Exactly. Good money for good brains.

They drink.

Thirty million! I mean . . .!

ROGER

Exactly.

STEPHEN

I'll tell you, neither I nor those above me are going to put up with it much longer. These people, Roger, these people are actively and wilfully deceiving the public. Do you take my point?

ROGER

I'd put the bastards up against a wall and shoot them.

STEPHEN

As a matter of fact, I've got a committee being set up to discuss that very thing.

ROGER

Really? Well done.

They drink.

Actually . . . I've heard that they're talking about forty million.

STEPHEN

What!

ROGER

And one or two of them . . . have taken it even further.

STEPHEN

What do you mean?

ROGER

Oh . . . you know . . . fifty . . . sixty . . . seventy . . .

STEPHEN

But that's almost the whole population!

ROGER

I know.

STEPHEN

Well I'm buggered.

ROGER

It's a bit of a bloody cheek, isn't it, Stephen?

STEPHEN

It's more than a bloody cheek, Roger.

ROGER

Indeed.

Pause.

STEPHEN

You know what I'm going to recommend we do with these people?

ROGER

What?

STEPHEN

I'm going to recommend that they be hung, drawn and quartered. I want to see the colour of their entrails.

ROGER

Same colour as the Red Flag, old boy.

STEPHEN

Quite.

They drink.

You see, what makes this whole business doubly disgusting is that the citizens of this country are behind us. They're ready to go with us on the twenty million basis. They're perfectly happy! And what are they faced with from these bastards? A deliberate attempt to subvert and undermine their security. And their faith.

ROGER *drinks and then looks at Stephen.*

ROGER
Give me another two, Stephen.

STEPHEN *stares at him.*

STEPHEN
Another two?

ROGER
Another two million. And I'll buy you another drink. Another two for another drink.

STEPHEN
(*Slowly*) No, no, Roger. It's twenty million. Dead.

ROGER
You mean precisely?

STEPHEN
I mean dead. Precisely.

Pause.

I want you to accept that figure.

Pause.

Accept the figure.

They stare at each other.

ROGER

Twenty million dead, precisely?

STEPHEN

Precisely.

ONE FOR THE ROAD

One for the Road was first performed at the Lyric Theatre Studio, Hammersmith, in March 1984, with the following cast:

NICOLAS	*mid 40s*	Alan Bates
VICTOR	30	Roger Lloyd Pack
GILA	30	Jenny Quayle
NICKY	7	Stephen Kember and Felix Yates

Directed by Harold Pinter

It was subsequently presented as part of the triple bill, *Other Places*, at the Duchess Theatre, London, on 7 March 1985, with the following cast:

NICOLAS	Colin Blakely
VICTOR	Roger Davidson
GILA	Rosie Kerslake
NICKY	Daniel Kipling and Simon Vyvyan

Directed by Kenneth Ives

NICOLAS *at his desk. He leans forward and speaks into a machine.*

NICOLAS

Bring him in.

He sits back. The door opens. VICTOR *walks in, slowly. His clothes are torn. He is bruised. The door closes behind him.*

Hello! Good morning. How are you? Let's not beat about the bush. Anything but that. *D'accord*? You're a civilised man, So am I. Sit down.

VICTOR *slowly sits.* NICOLAS *stands, walks over to him.*

What do you think this is? It's my finger. And this is my little finger. This is my big finger and this is my little finger. I wave my big finger in front of your eyes. Like this. And now I do the same with my little finger. I can also use both . . . at the same time. Like this. I can do absolutely anything I like. Do you think I'm mad? My mother did.

He laughs.

Do you think waving fingers in front of people's eyes is silly? I can see your point. You're a man of the highest intelligence. But would you take the same view if it was my boot – or my penis? Why am I so obsessed with eyes? Am I obsessed with eyes? Possibly. Not my eyes. Other people's eyes. The eyes of people who are brought to me here. They're so vulnerable. The soul shines through them. Are you a religious man? I am. Which side do you think God is on? I'm going to have a drink.

He goes to sideboard, pours whisky.

You're probably wondering where your wife is. She's in another room.

He drinks.

Good-looking woman.

He drinks.

God, that was good.

He pours another.

Don't worry, I can hold my booze.

He drinks.

You may have noticed I'm the chatty type. You probably think I'm part of a predictable, formal, long-established pattern; i.e. I chat away, friendly, insouciant,

224

I open the batting, as it were, in a light-hearted, even carefree manner, while another waits in the wings, silent, introspective, coiled like a puma. No, no. It's not quite like that. I run the place. God speaks through me. I'm referring to the Old Testament God, by the way, although I'm a long way from being Jewish. Everyone respects me here. Including you, I take it? I think that is the correct stance.

Pause.

Stand up.

VICTOR *stands.*

Sit down.

VICTOR *sits.*

Thank you so much.

Pause.

Tell me something . . .

Silence.

What a good-looking woman your wife is. You're a very lucky man. Tell me . . . one for the road, I think . . .

He pours whisky.

You do respect me, I take it?

He stands in front of VICTOR *and looks down at him.*
VICTOR *looks up.*

I would be right in assuming that?

Silence.

                    VICTOR
(*Quietly*) I don't know you.

                    NICOLAS
But you respect me.

                    VICTOR
I don't know you.

                    NICOLAS
Are you saying you don't respect me?

Pause.

Are you saying you would respect me if you knew me
better? Would you like to know me better?

Pause.

Would you like to know me better?

                    VICTOR
What I would like . . . has no bearing on the matter.

NICOLAS

Oh yes it has.

Pause.

I've heard so much about you. I'm terribly pleased to meet you. Well, I'm not sure that pleased is the right word. One has to be so scrupulous about language. Intrigued. I'm intrigued. Firstly because I've heard so much about you. Secondly because if you don't respect me you're unique. Everyone else knows the voice of God speaks through me. You're not a religious man, I take it?

Pause.

You don't believe in a guiding light?

Pause.

What then?

Pause.

So . . . morally . . . you flounder in wet shit. You know . . . like when you've eaten a rancid omelette.

Pause.

I think I deserve one for the road.

He pours, drinks.

Do you drink whisky?

Pause.

I hear you have a lovely house. Lots of books. Someone told me some of my boys kicked it around a bit. Pissed on the rugs, that sort of thing. I wish they wouldn't do that. I do really. But you know what it's like – they have such responsibilities – and they feel them – they are constantly present – day and night – these responsibilities – and so, sometimes, they piss on a few rugs. You understand. You're not a fool.

Pause.

Is your son all right?

VICTOR

I don't know.

NICOLAS

Oh, I'm sure he's all right. What age is he . . . seven . . . or thereabouts? Big lad, I'm told. Nevertheless, silly of him to behave as he did. But is he all right?

VICTOR

I don't know.

NICOLAS

Oh, I'm sure he's all right. Anyway, I'll have a word with him later and find out. He's somewhere on the second floor, I believe.

Pause.

Well now . . .

Pause.

What do you say? Are we friends?

Pause.

I'm prepared to be frank, as a true friend should. I love death. What about you?

Pause.

What about you? Do you love death? Not necessarily your own. Others'. The death of others. Do you love the death of others, or at any rate, do you love the death of others as much as I do?

Pause.

Are you always so dull? I understood you enjoyed the cut and thrust of debate.

Pause.

Death. Death. Death. Death. As has been noted by the most respected authorities, it is beautiful. The purest, most harmonious thing there is. Sexual intercourse is nothing compared to it.

He drinks.

Talking about sexual intercourse . . .

He laughs wildly, stops.

Does she . . . fuck? Or does she . . .? Or does she . . .
like . . . you know . . . what? What does she like? I'm
talking about your wife. Your *wife.*

Pause.

You know the old joke? Does she fuck?

Heavily, in another voice:

Does she fuck!

He laughs.

It's ambiguous, of course. It could mean she fucks like a
rabbit or she fucks not at all.

Pause.

Well, we're all God's creatures. Even your wife.

Pause.

There is only one obligation. *To be honest.* You have no
other obligation. Weigh that. In your mind. Do you
know the man who runs this country? No? Well, he's a
very nice chap. He took me aside the other day, last
Wednesday, I think it was, he took me aside, at a
reception, visiting dignitaries, he took *me* aside, *me*, and

he said to me, he said, in what I can only describe as a hoarse whisper, Nic, he said, Nic (that's my name), Nic, if you ever come across anyone whom you have good reason to believe is getting on my tits, tell them one thing, tell them honesty is the best policy. The cheese was superb. Goat. One for the road.

He pours.

Your wife and I had a very nice chat but I couldn't help noticing she didn't look her best. She's probably menstruating. Women do that.

Pause.

You know, old chap, I do love other things, apart from death. So many things. Nature. Trees, things like that. A nice blue sky. Blossom.

Pause.

Tell me . . . truly . . . are you beginning to love me?

Pause.

I think your wife is. Beginning. She is beginning to fall in love with me. On the brink . . . of doing so. The trouble is, I have rivals. Because everyone here has fallen in love with your wife. It's her eyes have beguiled them. What's her name? Gila . . . or something?

Pause.

231

Who would you prefer to be? You or me?

Pause.

I'd go for me if I were you. The trouble about you, although I grant your merits, is that you're on a losing wicket, while I can't put a foot wrong. Do you take my point? Ah God, let me confess, let me make a confession to you. I have never been more moved, in the whole of my life, as when – only the other day, last Friday, I believe – the man who runs this country announced to the country: We are all patriots, we are as one, we all share a common heritage. Except you, apparently.

Pause.

I feel a link, you see, a bond. I share a commonwealth of interest. I am not alone. I am not alone!

Silence.

                    VICTOR
Kill me.

                    NICOLAS
What?

                    VICTOR
Kill me.

NICOLAS *goes to* him, *puts his arm around him.*

NICOLAS

What's the matter?

Pause.

What in heaven's name is the matter?

Pause.

Mmmnnn?

Pause.

You're probably just hungry. Or thirsty. Let me tell you something. I hate despair. I find it intolerable. The stink of it gets up my nose. It's a blemish. Despair, old fruit, is a cancer. It should be castrated. Indeed I've often found that that works. Chop the balls off and despair goes out the window. You're left with a happy man. Or a happy woman. Look at me.

VICTOR *does so.*

Your soul shines out of your eyes.

Blackout.

Lights up. Afternoon.

NICOLAS *standing with a small boy.*

NICOLAS

What is your name?

233

NICKY

Nicky.

NICOLAS

Really? How odd.

Pause.

Do you like cowboys and Indians?

NICKY

Yes. A bit.

NICOLAS

What do you really like?

NICKY

I like aeroplanes.

NICOLAS

Real ones or toy ones?

NICKY

I like both kinds of ones.

NICOLAS

Do you?

Pause.

Why do you like aeroplanes?

Pause.

234

NICKY

Well . . . because they go so fast. Through the air. The real ones do.

NICOLAS

And the toy ones?

NICKY

I pretend they go as fast as the real ones do.

Pause.

NICOLAS

Do you like your mummy and daddy?

Pause.

Do you like your mummy and daddy?

NICKY

Yes.

NICOLAS

Why?

Pause.

Why?

Pause.

Do you find that a hard question to answer?

Pause.

NICKY

Where's mummy?

NICOLAS

You don't like your mummy and daddy?

NICKY

Yes, I do.

NICOLAS

Why?

Pause.

Would you like to be a soldier when you grow up?

NICKY

I don't mind.

NICOLAS

You don't? Good. You like soldiers. Good. But you spat at my soldiers and you kicked them. You attacked them.

NICKY

Were they your soldiers?

NICOLAS

They are your country's soldiers.

NICKY

I didn't like those soldiers.

NICOLAS

They don't like you either, my darling.

Blackout.

Lights up. Night.

NICOLAS *sitting.* GILA *standing. Her clothes are torn. She is bruised.*

NICOLAS

When did you meet your husband?

GILA

When I was eighteen.

NICOLAS

Why?

GILA

Why?

NICOLAS

Why?

GILA

I just met him.

NICOLAS

Why?

GILA

I didn't plan it.

NICOLAS

Why not?

GILA

I didn't know him.

NICOLAS

Why not?

Pause.

Why not?

GILA

I didn't know him.

NICOLAS

Why not?

GILA

I met him.

NICOLAS

When?

GILA

When I was eighteen.

NICOLAS

Why?

GILA

He was in the room.

NICOLAS

Room?

Pause.

Room?

GILA

The same room.

NICOLAS

As what?

GILA

As I was.

NICOLAS

As I was?

Pause.

GILA

(*Screaming*)

As I was!

NICOLAS

Room? What room?

GILA

A room.

NICOLAS

What room?

GILA

My father's room.

NICOLAS

Your father? What's your father got to do with it?

Pause.

Your *father*? How dare you? Fuckpig.

Pause.

Your father was a wonderful man. His country is proud
of him. He's dead. He was a man of honour. He's dead.
Are you prepared to insult the memory of your father?

Pause.

Are you prepared to defame, to debase, the memory of
your father? Your father fought for his country. I knew
him. I revered him. Everyone did. He believed in God.
He didn't *think*, like you shitbags. He *lived*. He lived.
He was iron and gold. He would die, he would die, he
would die, for his country, for his God. And he did die,
he died, he died, for his God. You turd. To spawn such
a daughter. What a fate. Oh, poor, perturbed spirit, to
be haunted for ever by such scum and spittle. How do

240

you dare speak of your father to me? I loved him, as if
he were my own father.

Silence.

Where did you meet your husband?

GILA

In a street.

NICOLAS

What were you doing there?

GILA

Walking.

NICOLAS

What was he doing?

GILA

Walking.

Pause.

I dropped something. He picked it up.

NICOLAS

What did you drop?

GILA

The evening paper.

NICOLAS

You were drunk.

Pause.

You were drugged.

Pause.

You had absconded from your hospital.

GILA

I was not in a hospital.

NICOLAS

Where are you now?

Pause.

Where are you now? Do you think you are in a hospital?

Pause.

Do you think we have nuns upstairs?

Pause.

What do we have upstairs?

GILA

No nuns.

NICOLAS

What do we have?

GILA

Men.

NICOLAS

Have they been raping you?

She stares at him.

How many times?

Pause.

How many times have you been raped?

Pause.

How many times?

He stands, goes to her, lifts his finger.

This is my big finger. And this is my little finger. Look. I wave them in front of your eyes. Like this. How many times have you been raped?

GILA

I don't know.

NICOLAS

And you consider yourself a reliable witness?

243

He goes to sideboard, pours drink, sits, drinks.

You're a lovely woman. Well, you were.

He leans back, drinks, sighs.

Your son is . . . seven. He's a little prick. You made him so. You have taught him to be so. You had a choice. You could have encouraged him to be a good person. Instead, you encouraged him to be a little prick. You encouraged him to spit, to strike at soldiers of honour, soldiers of God.

Pause.

Oh well . . . in one way I suppose it's academic.

Pause.

You're of no interest to me. I might even let you out of here, in due course. But I should think you might entertain us all a little more before you go.

Blackout.

Lights up. Night.

NICOLAS *standing.* VICTOR *sitting.* VICTOR *is tidily dressed.*

NICOLAS
How have you been? Surviving?

VICTOR

Yes.

NICOLAS

Yes?

VICTOR

Yes. Yes.

NICOLAS

Really? How?

VICTOR

Oh . . .

Pause.

NICOLAS

I can't hear you.

VICTOR

It's my mouth.

NICOLAS

Mouth?

VICTOR

Tongue.

NICOLAS

What's the matter with it?

Pause.

What about a drink? One for the road. What do you say to a drink?

He goes to bottle, pours two glasses, gives a glass to
VICTOR.

Drink up. It'll put lead in your pencil. And then we'll find someone to take it out.

He laughs.

We can do that, you know. We have a first-class brothel upstairs, on the sixth floor, chandeliers, the lot. They'll suck you in and blow you out in little bubbles. All volunteers. Their daddies are in our business. Which is, I remind you, to keep the world clean for God. Get me? Drink up. Drink up. Are you refusing to drink with me?

VICTOR *drinks. His head falls back.*

Cheers.

NICOLAS *drinks.*

You can go.

Pause.

You can leave. We'll meet again, I hope. I trust we will always remain friends. Go out. Enjoy life. Be good. Love your wife. She'll be joining you in about a week, by the way. If she feels up to it. Yes. I feel we've both benefited from our discussions.

VICTOR *mutters.*

What?

VICTOR *mutters.*

What?

VICTOR
My son.

NICOLAS
Your son? Oh, don't worry about him. He was a little prick.

VICTOR *straightens and stares at* NICOLAS.

Silence.

Blackout.

MOUNTAIN LANGUAGE

Mountain Language was first performed at the National Theatre on 20 October 1988. The cast was as follows:

YOUNG WOMAN	Miranda Richardson
ELDERLY WOMAN	Eileen Atkins
SERGEANT	Michael Gambon
OFFICER	Julian Wadham
GUARD	George Harris
PRISONER	Tony Haygarth
HOODED MAN	Alex Hardy
SECOND GUARD	Douglas McFerran

Directed by Harold Pinter
Designed by Michael Taylor

I
A Prison Wall

A line of women. An ELDERLY WOMAN, *cradling her hand. A basket at her feet. A* YOUNG WOMAN *with her arm around the* WOMAN'S *shoulders.*

A SERGEANT *enters, followed by an* OFFICER. *The* SERGEANT *points to the* YOUNG WOMAN.

SERGEANT
Name!

YOUNG WOMAN
We've given our names.

SERGEANT
Name?

YOUNG WOMAN
We've given our names.

SERGEANT
Name?

OFFICER (*To* SERGEANT)
Stop this shit. (*To* YOUNG WOMAN) Any complaints?

YOUNG WOMAN
She's been bitten.

OFFICER

Who?

Pause.

Who? Who's been bitten?

YOUNG WOMAN
She has. She has a torn hand. Look. Her hand has been bitten. This is blood.

SERGEANT (*To* YOUNG WOMAN)
What is your name?

OFFICER
Shut up.

He walks over to ELDERLY WOMAN.

What's happened to your hand? Has someone bitten your hand?

The WOMAN *slowly lifts her hand. He peers at it.*

Who did this? Who bit you?

YOUNG WOMAN
A Dobermann pinscher.

OFFICER
Which one?

Pause.

Which one?

Pause.

Sergeant!

SERGEANT *steps forward.*

SERGEANT
Sir!

OFFICER
Look at this woman's hand. I think the thumb is going to come off. (*To* ELDERLY WOMAN) Who did this?

She stares at him.

Who did this?

YOUNG WOMAN
A big dog.

OFFICER
What was his name?

Pause.

What was his *name*?

Pause.

Every dog has a *name*! They answer to their name. They are given a name by their parents and that is their name, that is their *name*! Before they bite, they *state* their name. It's a formal procedure. They state their name and then they bite. What was his name? If you tell me one of our dogs bit this woman without giving his name I will have that dog shot!

Silence.

Now – attention! Silence and attention! Sergeant!

SERGEANT

Sir?

OFFICER

Take any complaints.

SERGEANT

Any complaints? Has anyone got any complaints?

YOUNG WOMAN

We were told to be here at nine o'clock this morning.

SERGEANT

Right. Quite right. Nine o'clock this morning. Absolutely right. What's your complaint?

YOUNG WOMAN

We were here at nine o'clock this morning. It's now five o'clock. We have been standing here for eight hours. In the snow. Your men let Dobermann pinschers frighten us. One bit this woman's hand.

OFFICER

What was the name of this dog?

She looks at him.

YOUNG WOMAN

I don't know his name.

SERGEANT

With permission sir?

OFFICER

Go ahead.

SERGEANT

Your husbands, your sons, your fathers, these men you have been waiting to see, are shithouses. They are enemies of the State. They are shithouses.

The OFFICER steps towards the WOMEN.

OFFICER

Now hear this. You are mountain people. You hear me? Your language is dead. It is forbidden. It is not permitted to speak your mountain language in this place. You cannot speak your language to your men. It is not permitted. Do you understand? You may not speak it. It is outlawed. You may only speak the language of the capital. That is the only language permitted in this place. You will be badly punished if you attempt to speak your mountain language in this place. This is a military decree. It is the law. Your language is forbidden. It is dead. No one is allowed to speak your language. Your language no longer exists. Any questions?

YOUNG WOMAN

I do not speak the mountain language.

Silence. The OFFICER *and* SERGEANT *slowly circle her. The* SERGEANT *puts his hand on her bottom.*

SERGEANT

What language do you speak? What language do you speak with your arse?

OFFICER

These women, Sergeant, have as yet committed no crime. Remember that.

SERGEANT

Sir! But you're not saying they're without sin?

OFFICER

Oh, no. Oh, no, I'm not saying that.

SERGEANT

This one's full of it. She bounces with it.

OFFICER

She doesn't speak the mountain language.

The WOMAN *moves away from the* SERGEANT'S *hand and turns to face the two men.*

YOUNG WOMAN

My name is Sara Johnson. I have come to see my
husband. It is my right. Where is he?

OFFICER

Show me your papers.

She gives him a piece of paper. He examines it, turns to
SERGEANT.

He doesn't come from the mountains. He's in the wrong
batch.

SERGEANT

So is she. She looks like a fucking intellectual to me.

OFFICER

But you said her arse wobbled.

SERGEANT

Intellectual arses wobble the best.

Blackout.

2
Visitors Room

A PRISONER *sitting. The* ELDERLY WOMAN *sitting, with basket. A* GUARD *standing behind her.*

The PRISONER *and the* WOMAN *speak in a strong rural accent.*

Silence.

ELDERLY WOMAN

I have bread –

The GUARD *jabs her with a stick.*

GUARD

Forbidden. Language forbidden.

She looks at him. He jabs her.

It's forbidden. (*To* PRISONER) Tell her to speak the language of the capital.

PRISONER

She can't speak it.

Silence.

She doesn't speak it.

Silence.

ELDERLY WOMAN

I have apples –

The GUARD *jabs her and shouts.*

GUARD

Forbidden! Forbidden forbidden forbidden! Jesus
Christ! (*To* PRISONER) Does she understand what I'm
saying?

PRISONER

No.

GUARD

Doesn't she?

He bends over her.

Don't you?

She stares up at him.

PRISONER

She's old. She doesn't understand.

GUARD

Whose fault is that?

He laughs.

Not mine, I can tell you. And I'll tell you another thing.

I've got a wife and three kids. And you're all a pile of shit.

Silence.

PRISONER
I've got a wife and three kids.

GUARD
You've what?

Silence.

You've got what?

Silence.

What did you say to me? You've got what?

Silence.

You've got *what*?

He picks up the telephone and dials one digit.

Sergeant? I'm in the Blue Room . . . yes . . . I thought I should report, Sergeant . . . I think I've got a joker in here.

Lights to half. The figures are still.

Voices over:

ELDERLY WOMAN'S VOICE

The baby is waiting for you.

PRISONER'S VOICE

Your hand has been bitten.

ELDERLY WOMAN'S VOICE

They are all waiting for you.

PRISONER'S VOICE

They have bitten my mother's hand.

ELDERLY WOMAN'S VOICE

When you come home there will be such a welcome for you. Everyone is waiting for you. They're all waiting for you. They're all waiting to see you.

Lights up. The SERGEANT *comes in.*

SERGEANT

What joker?

Blackout.

3
Voice in the Darkness

SERGEANT'S VOICE

Who's that fucking woman? What's that fucking
woman doing here? Who let that fucking woman
through that fucking door?

SECOND GUARD'S VOICE

She's his wife.

Lights up.

A corridor.

A HOODED MAN *held up by the* GUARD *and the*
SERGEANT. *The* YOUNG WOMAN *at a distance from
them, staring at them.*

SERGEANT

What is this, a reception for Lady Duck Muck? Where's
the bloody Babycham? Who's got the bloody Babycham
for Lady Duck Muck?

He goes to the YOUNG WOMAN.

Hello, Miss. Sorry. A bit of a breakdown in
administration, I'm afraid. They've sent you through
the wrong door. Unbelievable. Someone'll be done for

262

this. Anyway, in the meantime, what can I do for you, dear lady, as they used to say in the movies?

Lights to half. The figures are still.

Voices over:

MAN'S VOICE

I watch you sleep. And then your eyes open. You look up at me above you and smile.

YOUNG WOMAN'S VOICE

You smile. When my eyes open I see you above me and smile.

MAN'S VOICE

We are out on a lake.

YOUNG WOMAN'S VOICE

It is spring.

MAN'S VOICE

I hold you. I warm you.

YOUNG WOMAN'S VOICE

When my eyes open I see you above me and smile.

Lights up. The HOODED MAN *collapses. The* YOUNG WOMAN *screams.*

YOUNG WOMAN

Charley!

The SERGEANT *clicks his fingers. The* GUARD *drags the* MAN *off.*

SERGEANT
Yes, you've come in the wrong door. It must be the computer. The computer's got a double hernia. But I'll tell you what – if you want any information on any aspect of life in this place we've got a bloke comes into the office every Tuesday week, except when it rains. He's right on top of his chosen subject. Give him a tinkle one of these days and he'll see you all right. His name is Dokes. Joseph Dokes.

YOUNG WOMAN
Can I fuck him? If I fuck him, will everything be all right?

SERGEANT
Sure. No problem.

YOUNG WOMAN
Thank you.

Blackout.

4
Visitors Room

GUARD, ELDERLY WOMAN, PRISONER.

Silence.

The PRISONER *has blood on his face. He sits trembling. The* WOMAN *is still. The* GUARD *is looking out of a window. He turns to look at them both.*

GUARD

Oh, I forgot to tell you. They've changed the rules. She can speak. She can speak in her own language. Until further notice.

PRISONER

She can speak?

GUARD

Yes. Until further notice. New rules.

Pause.

PRISONER

Mother, you can speak.

Pause.

Mother, I'm speaking to you. You see? We can speak.

265

You can speak to me in our own language.

She is still.

You can speak.

Pause.

Mother. Can you hear me? I am speaking to you in our own language.

Pause.

Do you hear me?

Pause.

It's our language.

Pause.

Can't you hear me? Do you hear me?

She does not respond.

Mother?

GUARD

Tell her she can speak in her own language. New rules. Until further notice.

PRISONER

Mother?

266

She does not respond. She sits still.

The PRISONER'*s trembling grows. He falls from the chair on to his knees, begins to gasp and shake violently.*

The SERGEANT *walks into the room and studies the* PRISONER *shaking on the floor.*

SERGEANT (*To* GUARD)
Look at this. You go out of your way to give them a helping hand and they fuck it up.

Blackout.

THE NEW WORLD ORDER

The New World Order was first performed on 19 July 1991 at the Royal Court Theatre Upstairs, London. The cast was as follows:

DES   Bill Paterson
LIONEL   Michael Byrne
BLINDFOLDED MAN Douglas McFerran

Directed by Harold Pinter
Designed by Ian MacNeil
Lighting by Kevin Sleep

A BLINDFOLDED MAN *sitting on a chair.*
Two men (DES *and* LIONEL) *looking at him.*

DES

Do you want to know something about this man?

LIONEL

What?

DES

He hasn't got any idea at all of what we're going to do
to him.

LIONEL

He hasn't, no.

DES

He hasn't, no. He hasn't got any idea at all about any
one of the number of things that we might do to him.

LIONEL

That we will do to him.

DES

That we will.

Pause.

271

Well, some of them. We'll do some of them.

LIONEL

Sometimes we do all of them.

DES

That can be counterproductive.

LIONEL

Bollocks.

They study the man. He is still.

DES

But anyway here he is, here he is sitting here, and he hasn't the faintest idea of what we might do to him.

LIONEL

Well, he probably has the *faintest* idea.

DES

A faint idea, yes. Possibly.

DES *bends over the man.*

Have you? What do you say?

He straightens.

Let's put it this way. He has *little* idea of what we might do to him, of what in fact we are about to do to him.

LIONEL

Or his wife. Don't forget his wife. He has little idea of
what we're about to do to his wife.

DES

Well, he probably has *some* idea, he's probably got
some idea. After all, he's read the papers.

LIONEL

What papers?

Pause.

DES

You're right there.

LIONEL

Who is this cunt anyway? What is he, some kind of
peasant – or a lecturer in theology?

DES

He's a lecturer in fucking peasant theology.

LIONEL

Is he? What about his wife?

DES

Women don't have theological inclinations.

LIONEL

Oh, I don't know. I used to discuss that question with
my mother – quite often.

DES

What question?

LIONEL

Oh you know, the theological aspirations of the female.

Pause.

DES

What did she say?

LIONEL

She said . . .

DES

What?

Pause.

LIONEL

I can't remember.

He turns to the man in the chair.

Motherfucker.

DES

Fuckpig.

They walk round the chair.

LIONEL

You know what I find really disappointing?

274

DES

What?

LIONEL

The level of ignorance that surrounds us. I mean, this prick here –

DES

You called him a cunt last time.

LIONEL

What?

DES

You called him a cunt last time. Now you call him a prick. How many times do I have to tell you? You've got to learn to define your terms and stick to them. You can't call him a cunt in one breath and a prick in the next. The terms are mutually contradictory. You'd lose face in any linguistic discussion group, take my tip.

LIONEL

Christ. Would I?

DES

Definitely. And you know what it means to you. You know what language means to you.

LIONEL

Yes, I do know.

DES

Yes, you do know. Look at this man here, for example.

He's a first-class example. See what I mean? Before he came in here he was a big shot, he never stopped shooting his mouth off, he never stopped questioning received ideas. Now – because he's apprehensive about what's about to happen to him – he's stopped all that, he's got nothing more to say, he's more or less called it a day. I mean once – not too long ago – this man was a man of conviction, wasn't he, a man of principle. Now he's just a prick.

LIONEL

Or a cunt.

DES

And we haven't even finished with him. We haven't begun.

LIONEL

No, we haven't even finished with him. We haven't even finished with him! Well, we haven't begun.

DES

And there's still his wife to come.

LIONEL

That's right. We haven't finished with him. We haven't even begun. And we haven't finished with his wife either.

DES

We haven't even begun.

LIONEL *put his hand over his face and sobs.*

DES

What are you crying about?

LIONEL

I love it. I love it. I love it.

He grasps DES*'s shoulder.*

Look. I have to tell you. I've got to tell you. There's no
one else I can tell.

DES

All right. Fine. Go on. What is it? Tell me.

Pause.

LIONEL

I feel so pure.

Pause.

DES

Well, you're right. You're right to feel pure. You know
why?

LIONEL

Why?

DES

Because you're keeping the world clean for democracy.

They look into each other's eyes.

I'm going to shake you by the hand.

DES *shakes* LIONEL'*s hand. He then gestures to the man in the chair with his thumb.*

And so will he . . . (*He looks at his watch*) . . . in about thirty-five minutes.

PARTY TIME

Party Time was first performed by the Almeida Theatre Company on 31 October 1991 at the Almeida Theatre, London. The cast was as follows:

TERRY, a man of forty	Peter Howitt
GAVIN, a man in his fifties	Barry Foster
DUSTY, a woman in her twenties	Cordelia Roche
MELISSA, a woman of seventy	Dorothy Tutin
LIZ, a woman in her thirties	Tacye Nichols
CHARLOTTE, a woman in her thirties	Nicola Pagett
FRED, a man in his forties	Roger Lloyd Pack
DOUGLAS, a man of fifty	Gawn Grainger
JIMMY, a young man	Harry Burton

Directed by Harold Pinter
Designed by Mark Thompson

Gavin's flat.

A large room. Sofas, armchairs, etc. People sitting, standing. A WAITER *with a drinks tray.*

Two doors. One door, which is never used, is half open, in a dim light.

GAVIN *and* TERRY *stand in foreground. The others sit in half-light, drinking.*

Spasmodic party music throughout the play.

TERRY
I tell you, it's got everything.

GAVIN
Has it?

TERRY
Oh, yes. Real class.

GAVIN
Really?

TERRY
Real class. I mean, what I mean to say, you play a game

of tennis, you have a beautiful swim, they've got a bar
right there –

GAVIN

Where?

TERRY

By the pool. You can have a fruit juice on the spot, no
extra charge, then they give you this fantastic hot
towel –

GAVIN

Hot?

TERRY

Wonderful. And I mean hot. I'm not joking.

GAVIN

Like the barber.

TERRY

Barber?

GAVIN

In the barber shop. When I was a boy.

TERRY

Oh yes?

Pause.

What do you mean?

GAVIN

They used to put a hot towel over your face, you see,
over your nose and eyes. I had it done thousands of
times. It got rid of all the blackheads, all the blackheads
on your face.

TERRY

Blackheads?

GAVIN

It burnt them out. The towels, you see, were as hot as
you could stand. That's what the barber used to say:
'Hot enough for you, sir?' It burnt all the blackheads
out of your skin.

Pause.

I was born in the West Country, of course. So I could be
talking only of West Country barber shops. But on the
other hand I'm pretty sure that hot towels for
blackheads were used in barber shops throughout the
land in those days. Yes, I believe it was common
practice in those days.

TERRY

Well, I'm sure it was. I'm sure it was. But no, these
towels I'm talking about are big bath towels, towels for
the body, I'm just talking about pure comfort, that's
why I'm telling you, the place has got real class, it's got
everything. Mind you, there's a waiting list as long as –
I mean you've got to be proposed and seconded, and
then they've got to check you out, they don't let any old
spare bugger in there, why should they?

283

GAVIN

Quite right.

TERRY

But of course it goes without saying that someone like yourself would be warmly welcome – as an honorary member.

GAVIN

How kind.

DUSTY *walks through the door and joins them.*

DUSTY

Did you hear what's happened to Jimmy? What's happened to Jimmy?

TERRY

Nothing's happened.

DUSTY

Nothing?

GAVIN

Nobody is discussing this. Nobody's discussing it, sweetie. Do you follow me? Nothing's happened to Jimmy. And if you're not a good girl I'll spank you.

DUSTY

What's going on?

TERRY

Tell him about the new club. I've just been telling him about the club. She's a member.

GAVIN

What's it like?

DUSTY

Oh, it's beautiful. It's got everything. It's beautiful. The lighting's wonderful. Isn't it? Did you tell him about the alcoves?

TERRY

Well, there's a bar, you see, with glass alcoves, looking out to under the water.

DUSTY

People swim at you, you see, while you're having a drink.

TERRY

Lovely girls.

DUSTY

And men.

TERRY

Mostly girls.

DUSTY

Did you tell him about the food?

TERRY

The cannelloni is brilliant.

DUSTY

It's first class. The food is really first class.

TERRY

They even do chopped liver.

GAVIN

You couldn't describe that as a local dish.

MELISSA *comes through the door and joins them.*

MELISSA

What on earth's going on out there? It's like the Black Death.

TERRY

What is?

MELISSA

The town's dead. There's nobody on the streets, there's not a soul in sight, apart from some . . . soldiers. My driver had to stop at a . . . you know . . . what do you call it? . . . a roadblock. We had to say who we were . . . it really was a trifle . . .

GAVIN

Oh, there's just been a little . . . you know . . .

TERRY

Nothing in it. Can I introduce you? Gavin White – our host. Dame Melissa.

GAVIN

So glad you could come.

TERRY

What are you drinking?

The WAITER *approaches.*

Have a glass of wine.

He hands MELISSA *a glass.*

DUSTY

I keep hearing all these things. I don't know what to believe.

MELISSA
(*to* GAVIN)

What a lovely party.

TERRY
(*to* DUSTY)

What did you say?

DUSTY

I said I don't know what to believe.

TERRY

You don't have to believe anything. You just have to

shut up and mind your own business, how many times do I have to tell you? You come to a lovely party like this, all you have to do is shut up and enjoy the hospitality and mind your own fucking business. How many more times do I have to tell you? You keep hearing all these things. You keep hearing all these things spread by pricks about pricks. What's it got to do with you?

Lights up on LIZ *and* CHARLOTTE, *sitting on a sofa.*

LIZ

So beautiful. The mouth, really. And of course the eyes.

CHARLOTTE

Yes.

LIZ

Not to mention his hands. I'll tell you, I would have killed –

CHARLOTTE

I could see –

LIZ

But that bitch had her legs all over him.

CHARLOTTE

I know.

LIZ

I thought she was going to crush him to death.

288

CHARLOTTE

Unbelievable.

LIZ

Her skirt was right up to her neck – did you see?

CHARLOTTE

So barefaced –

LIZ

Next minute she's lugging him up the stairs.

CHARLOTTE

I saw.

LIZ

But as he was going, do you know what he did?

CHARLOTTE

What?

LIZ

He looked at me.

CHARLOTTE

Did he?

LIZ

I swear it. As he was being lugged out he looked back, he looked back, I swear, at me, like a wounded deer, I shall never, as long as I live, forget it, I shall never forget that look.

CHARLOTTE

How beautiful.

LIZ

I could have cut her throat, that nymphomaniac slut.

CHARLOTTE

Yes, but think what happened. Think of the wonderful
side of it. Because for you it was love, it was falling in
love. That's what it was, wasn't it? You fell in love.

LIZ

I did. You're right. I fell in love. I am in love. I haven't
slept all night, I'm in love.

CHARLOTTE

How many times does that happen? That's the point.
How often does it really happen? How often does
anyone experience such a thing?

LIZ

Yes, you're right. That's what happened to me. That is
what has happened – to me.

CHARLOTTE

That's why you're in such pain.

LIZ

Yes, because that bigtitted tart –

CHARLOTTE

Raped the man you love.

LIZ

Yes she did. That's what she did. She raped my beloved.

Lights up on FRED *and* DOUGLAS, *drinking.*

FRED

We've got to make it work.

DOUGLAS

What?

FRED

The country.

Pause.

DOUGLAS

You've brought the house down with that one, Fred.

FRED

But that's what matters. That's what matters. Doesn't it?

DOUGLAS

Oh, it matters. It matters. I should say it matters. All this fucking-about has to stop.

FRED

You mean it?

DOUGLAS

I mean it all right.

FRED

I admire people like you.

DOUGLAS

So do I.

FRED *clenches his fist.*

FRED

A bit of that.

DOUGLAS *clenches his fist.*

DOUGLAS

A bit of that.

Pause.

FRED

How's it going tonight?

DOUGLAS

Like clockwork. Look. Let me tell you something. We want peace. We want peace and we're going to get it.

FRED

Quite right.

DOUGLAS

We want peace and we're going to get it. But we want that peace to be cast iron. No leaks. No draughts. Cast iron. Tight as a drum. That's the kind of peace we want

292

and that's the kind of peace we're going to get. A cast-iron peace.

He clenches his fist.

Like this.

FRED

You know, I really admire people like you.

DOUGLAS

So do I.

Lights up on MELISSA, DUSTY, TERRY *and* GAVIN.

MELISSA
(*to* DUSTY)

How sweet of you to say so.

DUSTY

But you do have a really wonderful figure. Honestly. Doesn't she?

TERRY

I've known this lady for years. Haven't I? How many years have I known you? Years. And she's always looked the same. Haven't you? She's always looked the same. Hasn't she?

GAVIN

Has she?

DUSTY

Always. Haven't you?

TERRY

She has. Isn't that right?

MELISSA

Oh, you're joking.

TERRY

Not me. I never joke. Have you ever heard me crack a
joke?

MELISSA

No, if I still look all right, it's probably because I've just
joined this new club – (*To* GAVIN) Do you know it?

TERRY

We were just telling him. We were just telling him all
about it.

MELISSA

Oh, were you?

GAVIN

Just now, yes. Sounds delightful. You're a member, are
you?

MELISSA

Oh yes. I think it's saved my life. The swimming. Why
don't you join? Do you play tennis?

GAVIN

I'm a golfer. I play golf.

MELISSA

What else do you do?

GAVIN
(*smiling*)
I don't understand what you mean.

TERRY

What else does he do? He doesn't do anything else. He
plays golf. That's what he does. That's all he does. He
plays golf.

GAVIN

Well . . . I do sail. I do own a boat.

DUSTY

I love boats.

TERRY

What?

DUSTY

I love boats. I love boating.

TERRY

Boating. Did you hear that?

DUSTY

I love cooking on boats.

TERRY

The only thing she doesn't like on boats is being fucked
on boats. That's what she doesn't like.

MELISSA

That's funny. I thought everyone liked that.

Silence.

DUSTY

Does anyone know what's happened to my brother
Jimmy?

TERRY

I don't know what it is. Perhaps she's deaf or perhaps
my voice isn't strong enough or distinct enough. What
do you think, folks? Perhaps there's something faulty
with my diction. I'm forced to float all these possibilities
because I thought I had said that we don't discuss this
question of what has happened to Jimmy, that it's not
up for discussion, that it's not on anyone's agenda. I
thought I had already made that point quite clearly. But
perhaps my voice isn't strong enough or perhaps my
articulation isn't good enough or perhaps she's deaf.

DUSTY

It's on my agenda.

TERRY

What did you say?

DUSTY

I said it's on my agenda.

TERRY

No no, you've got it wrong there, old darling. What you've got wrong there, old darling, what you've got totally wrong, is that you don't have any agenda. Got it? You have no agenda. Absolutely the opposite is the case. (*To the others*) I'm going to have to give her a real talking to when I get her home, I can see that.

GAVIN

So odd, the number of men who can't control their wives.

TERRY

What?

GAVIN
(*to* MELISSA)

It's the root of so many ills, you know. Uncontrollable wives.

MELISSA

Yes, I know what you mean.

TERRY

What are you saying to me?

GAVIN
(*to* MELISSA)

I went for a walk in the woods the other day. I had no idea how many squirrels were still left in this country. I find them such vivacious creatures, quite enchanting.

MELISSA

I used to love them as a girl.

GAVIN

Did you really? What about hawks?

MELISSA

Oh I loved hawks too. And eagles. But certainly hawks. The kestrel. The way it flew, and hovered, over my valley. It made me cry. I still cry.

The lights in the room dim.

The light beyond the open door gradually intensifies. It burns into the room.

The door light fades down. The room lights come up on DOUGLAS, FRED, LIZ *and* CHARLOTTE.

DOUGLAS

Oh, have you met my wife?

FRED
(*to* LIZ)

How do you do?

LIZ

This is Charlotte.

FRED

We've met before.

LIZ

You've met before?

CHARLOTTE

Oh yes. We've met. He gave me a leg up in life.

DOUGLAS

Did you really? How exciting.

FRED

It was.

DOUGLAS

Was it exciting for you too? To be given a leg up?

CHARLOTTE

Mmmmnnn. Yes. Oh, yes. I'm still trembling.

DOUGLAS

How exciting.

LIZ

I think this is such a gorgeous party. Don't you? I mean
I just think it's such a gorgeous party. Don't you? I
think it's such fun. I love the fact that people are so well
dressed. Casual but good. Do you know what I mean?
Is it silly to say I feel proud? I mean to be part of the
society of beautifully dressed people? Oh God I don't
know, elegance, style, grace, taste, don't these words,
these concepts, mean anything any more? I'm not alone,
am I, in thinking them incredibly important? Anyway I
love everything that flows. I can't tell you how happy I
feel.

FRED
(*to* CHARLOTTE)

You married someone. I've forgotten who it was.

Silence.

CHARLOTTE

He died.

Silence.

DOUGLAS

If you're free this summer do come to our island. We take an island for the summer. Do come. There's more or less nobody there. Just a few local people who do us proud. Terribly civil. Everything works. I have my own generator. But the storms are wild, aren't they darling? If you like storms. Siroccos. Makes you feel alive. Truly alive. Makes the old pulse go rat-at-tat-tat. God it can be wild, can't it darling? Makes the old pulse go rat-at-tat-tat. Raises the ante. You know. Gets the blood up. Actually, when I'm out there on the island I feel ten years younger. I could take anyone on. Man, woman or child, what?

He laughs.

I could take a wild animal on. But then when the storm is over and night falls and the moon is out in all its glory and all you're left with is the rhythm of the sea, of the waves, you know what God intended for the human race, you know what paradise is.

Lights up on TERRY *and* DUSTY, *in a corner of the room.*

TERRY

Are you mad? Do you know what that man is?

DUSTY

Yes, I think I know what that man is.

TERRY

You don't know what he is. You have no idea. You don't know what his position is. You have simply no idea. You simply have no idea.

DUSTY

He has lovely manners. He seems to come from another world. A courteous, caring world. He'll send me flowers in the morning.

TERRY

No he bloody won't. Oh no he bloody won't.

DUSTY

Poor darling, are you upset? Have I let you down? I've let you down. And I've always tried to be such a good wife. Such a good wife.

They stare at each other.

Perhaps you'll kill me when we get home? Do you think you will? Do you think you'll put an end to it? Do you think there is an end to it? What do you think? Do you think that if you put an end to me that would be the end of everything for everyone? Will everything and everyone die with me?

TERRY

Yes, you're all going to die together, you and all your lot.

DUSTY

How are you going to do it? Tell me.

TERRY

Easy. We've got dozens of options. We could suffocate every single one of you at a given signal or we could shove a broomstick up each individual arse at another given signal or we could poison all the mother's milk in the world so that every baby would drop dead before it opened its perverted bloody mouth.

DUSTY

But will it be fun for me? Will it be fun?

TERRY

You'll love it. But I'm not going to tell you which method we'll use. I just want you to have a lot of sexual anticipation. I want you to look forward to whatever the means employed with a lot of sexual anticipation.

DUSTY

But you still love me?

TERRY

Of course I love you. You're the mother of my children.

DUSTY

Oh incidentally, what's happened to Jimmy?

Lights up on FRED *and* CHARLOTTE.

FRED

Such a long time.

CHARLOTTE

Such a long time.

FRED

Isn't it?

CHARLOTTE

Oh, yes. Ages.

FRED

You're looking as beautiful as ever.

CHARLOTTE

So are you.

FRED

Me? Not me.

CHARLOTTE

Oh, you are. Well, in a manner of speaking.

FRED

What do you mean, in a manner of speaking?

CHARLOTTE

Oh, I meant you look as beautiful as ever.

FRED

But I never was beautiful. In any way.

CHARLOTTE

No, that's true. You weren't. In any way at all. I've been talking shit. In a manner of speaking.

FRED

Your language was always deplorable.

CHARLOTTE

Yes. Appalling.

FRED

Are you enjoying the party?

CHARLOTTE

Best party I've been to in years.

Pause.

FRED

You said your husband died.

CHARLOTTE

My what?

FRED

Your husband.

CHARLOTTE

Oh my husband. Oh yes. That's right. He died.

FRED

Was it a long illness?

CHARLOTTE

Short.

FRED

Ah.

Pause.

Quick then.

CHARLOTTE

Quick, yes. Short and quick.

Pause.

FRED

Better that way.

CHARLOTTE

Really?

FRED

I would have thought.

CHARLOTTE

Ah. I see. Yes.

Pause.

Better for who?

FRED

What?

CHARLOTTE

You said it would be better. Better for who?

FRED

For you.

CHARLOTTE *laughs.*

CHARLOTTE

Yes! I'm glad you didn't say him.

FRED

Well, I could say him. A quick death must be better
than a slow one. It stands to reason.

CHARLOTTE

No it doesn't.

Pause.

Anyway, I'll bet it can be quick and slow at the same
time. I bet it can. I bet death can be both things at the
same time. Oh by the way, he wasn't ill.

Pause.

FRED

You're still very beautiful.

CHARLOTTE

I think there's something going on in the street.

FRED

What?

CHARLOTTE

I think there's something going on in the street.

FRED

Leave the street to us.

CHARLOTTE

Who's us?

FRED

Oh, just us . . . you know.

She stares at him.

CHARLOTTE

God, your looks! No, seriously. You're still so
handsome! How do you do it? What's your diet?
What's your regime? What *is* your regime by the way?
What do you do to keep yourself so . . . I don't know
. . . so . . . oh, I don't know . . . so trim, so fit?

FRED

I lead a clean life.

DOUGLAS *and* LIZ *join them.*

CHARLOTTE
(*to* DOUGLAS)

Do you too?

DOUGLAS

Do I what?

CHARLOTTE

Fred says he looks so fit and so . . . handsome . . . because he leads a clean life. What about you?

DOUGLAS

I lead an incredibly clean life. It doesn't make me handsome but it makes me happy.

LIZ

And it makes me happy too. So happy.

DOUGLAS

Even though I'm not handsome?

LIZ

But you are. You are. Isn't he? He is. You are. Isn't he?

DOUGLAS *puts his arm around her.*

DOUGLAS

When we were first married we lived in a two-roomed flat. I was – I'll be frank – I was a traveller, a commercial traveller, a salesman – it's true, that's what I was and I don't deny it – and travel I did. Didn't I?

Travel I did. Because my little girl here had given birth to twins.

He laughs.

Can you believe it? Twins. I had to slave my guts out, I can tell you. But this girl here, this little girl here, do you know what she did? She looked after those twins all by herself! No maid, no help, nothing. She did it herself – all by herself. And when I got back from my travelling I would find the flat immaculate, the twins bathed and in bed, tucked up in bed, fast asleep, my wife looking beautiful and my dinner in the oven.

FRED *applauds.*

And that's why we're still together.

He kisses LIZ *on the cheek.*

That's why we're still together.

The lights in the room dim.

The light beyond the open door gradually intensifies. It burns into the room.

The door light fades down. The room lights come up on TERRY, DUSTY, GAVIN, MELISSA, FRED, CHARLOTTE, DOUGLAS *and* LIZ.

TERRY
The thing is, it is actually real value for money. Now

this is a very, very unusual thing. It is an extremely
unusual thing these days to find that you are getting real
value for money. You take your hand out of your
pocket and you put your money down and you know
what you're getting. And what you're getting is
absolutely gold-plated service. Gold-plated service in all
departments. You've got real catering. You've got
catering on all levels. You've not only got very good
catering in itself – you know, food, that kind of thing –
and napkins – you know, all that, wonderful, first rate –
but you've also got artistic catering – you actually have
an atmosphere – in this club – which is catering
artistically for its clientele. I'm referring to the kind of
light, the kind of paint, the kind of music, the club
offers. I'm talking about a truly warm and harmonious
environment. You won't find voices raised in our club.
People don't do vulgar and sordid and offensive things.
And if they do we kick them in the balls and chuck
them down the stairs with no trouble at all.

MELISSA
Can I subscribe to all that has just been said?

Pause.

I would like to subscribe to all that has just been said. I
would like to add my voice. I have belonged to many
tennis and swimming clubs. Many tennis and swimming
clubs. And at some of these clubs I first met some of my
dearest friends. All of them are now dead. Every friend I
ever had. Or ever met. Is dead. They are all of them
dead. Every single one of them. I have absolutely not
one left. None are left. Nothing is left. What was it all

for? The tennis and the swimming clubs? What was it all for? What?

Silence.

But the clubs died too and rightly so. I mean there is a distinction to be made. My friends went the way of all flesh and I don't regret their passing. They weren't my friends anyway. I couldn't stand half of them. But the clubs! The clubs died, the swimming and the tennis clubs died because they were based on ideas which had no moral foundation, no moral foundation whatsoever. But *our* club, *our* club – is a club which is activated, which is inspired by a moral sense, a moral awareness, a set of moral values which is – I have to say – unshakeable, rigorous, fundamental, constant. Thank you.

Applause.

GAVIN
Yes, I'm terribly glad you've said all that. (*To the others*) Aren't you?

DOUGLAS
First rate.

LIZ
So moving.

TERRY
Fantastic.

FRED

Right on the nail.

CHARLOTTE

So true.

DUSTY

Oh yes.

She claps her hands.

Oh yes.

DOUGLAS

Absolutely first rate.

GAVIN

Yes, it was first rate. And it desperately needed saying. And how splendid that it was said tonight, at such an enjoyable party, in such congenial company. I must say I speak as a very happy host. And by the way, I'll really have to join this wonderful club of yours, won't I?

TERRY

You're elected forthwith. You're an honorary member. As of today.

Laughter and applause.

GAVIN

Thank you very much indeed. Now I believe one or two of our guests encountered traffic problems on their way here tonight. I apologise for that, but I would like to assure you that all such problems and all related problems will be resolved very soon. Between ourselves, we've had a bit of a round-up this evening. This round-up is coming to an end. In fact normal services will be resumed shortly. That is, after all, our aim. Normal service. We, if you like, insist on it. We will insist on it. We do. That's all we ask, that the service this country provides will run on normal, secure and legitimate paths and that the ordinary citizen be allowed to pursue his labours and his leisure in peace. Thank you all so much for coming here tonight. It's been really lovely to see you, quite smashing.

The room lights go down.

The light from the door intensifies, burning into the room.

Everyone is still, in silhouette.

A man comes out of the light and stands in the doorway. He is thinly dressed.

JIMMY

Sometimes I hear things. Then it's quiet.

I had a name. It was Jimmy. People called me Jimmy. That was my name.

Sometimes I hear things. Then everything is quiet. When everything is quiet I hear my heart.

When the terrible noises come I don't hear anything.
Don't hear don't breathe am blind.

Then everything is quiet. I hear a heartbeat. It is
probably not my heartbeat. It is probably someone
else's heartbeat.

What am I?

Sometimes a door bangs, I hear voices, then it stops.
Everything stops. It all stops. It all closes. It closes
down. It shuts. It all shuts. It shuts down. It shuts. I see
nothing at any time any more. I sit sucking the dark.

It's what I have. The dark is in my mouth and I suck it.
It's the only thing I have. It's mine. It's my own. I suck
it.

MOONLIGHT

CHARACTERS

ANDY, a man in his fifties
BEL, a woman of fifty
JAKE, a man of twenty-eight
FRED, a man of twenty-seven
MARIA, a woman of fifty
RALPH, a man in his fifties
BRIDGET, a girl of sixteen

THREE MAIN PLAYING AREAS:

1. Andy's bedroom – well furnished.
2. Fred's bedroom – shabby.

(*These rooms are in different locations.*)

3. An area in which Bridget appears, through which Andy moves at night and where Jake, Fred and Bridget play their scene.

Moonlight was first performed at the Almeida Theatre, London, on 7 September 1993. The cast was as follows:

ANDY   Ian Holm
BEL   Anna Massey
JAKE   Douglas Hodge
FRED   Michael Sheen
MARIA   Jill Johnson
RALPH   Edward de Souza
BRIDGET   Claire Skinner

Directed by David Leveaux
Designed by Bob Crowley

BRIDGET *in faint light.*

BRIDGET

I can't sleep. There's no moon. It's so dark. I think I'll
go downstairs and walk about. I won't make a noise.
I'll be very quiet. Nobody will hear me. It's so dark and
I know everything is more silent when it's dark. But I
don't want anyone to know I'm moving about in the
night. I don't want to wake my father and mother.
They're so tired. They have given so much of their life
for me and for my brothers. All their life, in fact. All
their energies and all their love. They need to sleep in
peace and wake up rested. I must see that this happens.
It is my task. Because I know that when they look at me
they see that I am all they have left of their life.

Andy's bedroom.
ANDY *in bed.* BEL *sitting.*
She is doing embroidery.

ANDY

Where are the boys? Have you found them?

BEL

I'm trying.

ANDY

You've been trying for weeks. And failing. It's enough
to make the cat laugh. Do we have a cat?

BEL

We do.

ANDY

Is it laughing?

BEL

Fit to bust.

ANDY

What at? Me, I suppose.

BEL

Why would your own dear cat laugh at you? That cat
who was your own darling kitten when she was young
and so were you, that cat you have so dandled and
patted and petted and loved, why should she, how
could she, laugh at her master? It's not remotely
credible.

ANDY

But she's laughing at someone?

BEL

She's laughing at me. At my ineptitude. At my failure to
find the boys, at my failure to bring the boys to their
father's deathbed.

ANDY

Well that's more like it. You are the proper target for a cat's derision. And how I loved you.

Pause.

What a wonderful woman you were. You had such a great heart. You still have, of course. I can hear it from here. Banging away.

Pause.

BEL

Do you feel anything? What do you feel? Do you feel hot? Or cold? Or both? What do you feel? Do you feel cold in your legs? Or hot? What about your fingers? What are they? Are they cold? Or hot? Or neither cold nor hot?

ANDY

Is this a joke? My God, she's taking the piss out of me. My own wife. On my deathbed. She's as bad as that fucking cat.

BEL

Perhaps it's my convent school education but the term 'taking the piss' does leave me somewhat nonplussed.

ANDY

Nonplussed! You've never been nonplussed in the whole of your voracious, lascivious, libidinous life.

BEL

You may be dying but that doesn't mean you have to be *totally* ridiculous.

ANDY

Why am I dying, anyway? I've never harmed a soul. You don't die if you're good. You die if you're bad.

BEL

We girls were certainly aware of the verb 'to piss', oh yes, in the sixth form, certainly. I piss, you piss, she pisses, et cetera.

ANDY

We girls! Christ!

BEL

The term 'taking the piss', however, was not known to us.

ANDY

It means mockery! It means to mock. It means mockery! Mockery! Mockery!

BEL

Really? How odd. Is there a rational explanation to this?

ANDY

Rationality went down the drain donkey's years ago and hasn't been seen since. All that famous rationality of yours is swimming about in waste disposal turdology. It's burping and farting away in the cesspit for ever and ever. That's destiny speaking, sweetheart! That was always the destiny of your famous rational intelligence, to choke to death in sour cream and pigswill.

BEL

Oh do calm down, for goodness sake.

ANDY

Why? Why?

Pause.

What do you mean?

Fred's bedroom.
FRED *in bed.* JAKE *in to him.*

JAKE

Brother.

FRED

Brother.

JAKE *sits by the bed.*

JAKE

And how is my little brother?

FRED

Cheerful though gloomy. Uneasily poised.

JAKE

All will be well. And all manner of things shall be well.

Pause.

FRED

What kind of holiday are you giving me this year? Art or the beach?

JAKE

I would think a man of your calibre needs a bit of both.

FRED

Or nothing of either.

JAKE

It's very important to keep your pecker up.

FRED

How far up?

JAKE

Well . . . for example . . . how high is a Chinaman?

FRED

Quite.

JAKE

Exactly.

Pause.

FRED

You were writing poems when you were a mere child,
isn't that right?

JAKE

I was writing poems before I could read.

FRED

Listen. I happen to know that you were writing poems
before you could speak.

JAKE

Listen! I was writing poems before I was born.

FRED

So you would say you were the real thing?

JAKE

The authentic article.

FRED

Never knowingly undersold.

JAKE

Precisely.

Silence.

FRED

Listen. I've been thinking about the whole caboodle. I'll
tell you what we need. We need capital.

JAKE

I've got it.

FRED

You've got it?

JAKE

I've got it.

FRED

Where did you find it?

JAKE

Divine right.

FRED

Christ.

JAKE

Exactly.

FRED

You're joking.

JAKE

No, no, my father weighed it all up carefully the day I was born.

FRED

Oh, your father? Was he the one who was sleeping with your mother?

JAKE

He weighed it all up. He weighed up all the pros and
cons and then without further ado he called a meeting.
He called a meeting of the trustees of his estate, you see,
to discuss all these pros and cons. My father was a very
thorough man. He invariably brought the meetings in
on time and under budget and he always kept a weather
eye open for blasphemy, gluttony and buggery.

FRED

He was a truly critical force?

JAKE

He was not in it for pleasure or glory. Let me make that
quite clear. Applause came not his way. Nor did he seek
it. Gratitude came not his way. Nor did he seek it.
Masturbation came not his way. Nor did he seek it. I'm
sorry – I meant approbation came not his way –

FRED

Oh, didn't it really?

JAKE

Nor did he seek it.

Pause.

I'd like to apologise for what I can only describe as a
lapse in concentration.

FRED

It can happen to anybody.

Pause.

JAKE

My father adhered strictly to the rule of law.

FRED

Which is not a very long way from the rule of thumb.

JAKE

Not as the crow flies, no.

FRED

But the trustees, I take it, could not, by any stretch of the imagination, be described as a particularly motley crew?

JAKE

Neither motley nor random. They were kept, however, under strict and implacable scrutiny. They were allowed to go to the lavatory just one and a half times a session. They evacuated to a timeclock.

FRED

And the motion was carried?

JAKE

The motion was carried, nine votes to four, Jorrocks abstaining.

FRED

Not a pretty sight, by the sound of it.

JAKE

The vicar stood up. He said that it was a very unusual
thing, a truly rare and unusual thing, for a man in the
prime of his life to leave – without codicil or reservation –
his personal fortune to his newborn son the very day of
that baby's birth – before the boy had had a chance to say a
few words or aspire to the unknowable or cut for partners
or cajole the japonica or tickle his arse with a feather –

FRED

Whose arse?

JAKE

It was an act, went on the vicar, which, for sheer
undaunted farsightedness, unflinching moral resolve,
stern intellectual vision, classic philosophical
detachment, passionate religious fervour, profound
emotional intensity, bloodtingling spiritual ardour,
spellbinding metaphysical chutzpah – stood alone.

FRED

Tantamount to a backflip in the lotus position.

JAKE

It was an act, went on the vicar, without a vestige of lust
but with any amount of bucketfuls of lustre.

FRED

So the vicar was impressed?

JAKE

The only one of the trustees not impressed was my
Uncle Rufus.

329

FRED

Now you're telling me you had an uncle called Rufus. Is that what you're telling me?

JAKE

Uncle Rufus was not impressed.

FRED

Why not? Do I know the answer? I think I do. I think I do. Do I?

Pause.

JAKE

I think you do.

FRED

I think so too. I think I do.

JAKE

I think so too.

Pause.

FRED

The answer is that your father was just a little bit short of a few krugerrands.

JAKE

He'd run out of pesetas in a pretty spectacular fashion.

FRED

He had, only a few nights before, dropped a packet on
the pier at Bognor Regis.

JAKE

Fishing for tiddlers.

FRED

His casino life had long been a lost horizon.

JAKE

The silver pail was empty.

FRED

As was the gold.

JAKE

Nary an emerald.

FRED

Nary a gem.

JAKE

Gemless in Wall Street –

FRED

To the bank with fuck-all.

JAKE

Yes – it must and will be said – the speech my father
gave at that trustees meeting on that wonderfully soft
summer morning in the Cotswolds all those years ago

was the speech either of a mountebank – a child – a
shyster – a fool – a villain –

FRED

Or a saint.

MARIA *to them.* JAKE *stands.*

MARIA

Do you remember me? I was your mother's best friend.
You're both so tall. I remember you when you were
little boys. And Bridget of course. I once took you all to
the Zoo, with your father. We had tea. Do you
remember? I used to come to tea, with your mother. We
drank so much tea in those days! My three are all in
terribly good form. Sarah's doing marvellously well and
Lucien's thriving at the Consulate and as for Susannah,
there's no stopping her. But don't you remember the
word games we all used to play? Then we'd walk across
the Common. That's where we met Ralph. He was
refereeing a football match. He did it, oh I don't know,
with such aplomb, such command. Your mother and I
were so . . . impressed. He was always ahead of the
game. He knew where the ball was going before it was
kicked. Osmosis. I think that's the word. He's still as
osmotic as anyone I've ever come across. Much more
so, of course. Most people have no osmotic quality
whatsoever. But of course in those days – I won't deny it
– I had a great affection for your father. And so had
your mother – for your father. Your father possessed
little in the way of osmosis but nor did he hide his
blushes under a barrel. I mean he wasn't a pretender, he
didn't waste precious time. And how he danced. How

he danced. One of the great waltzers. An elegance and grace long gone. A firmness and authority so seldom encountered. And he looked you directly in the eye. Unwavering. As he swirled you across the floor. A rare gift. But I was young in those days. So was your mother. Your mother was marvellously young and quickening every moment. I – I must say – particularly when I saw your mother being swirled across the floor by your father – felt buds breaking out all over the place. I thought I'd go mad.

Andy's room.
ANDY *and* BEL.

ANDY

I'll tell you something about me. I sweated over a hot desk all my working life and nobody ever found a flaw in my working procedures. Nobody ever uncovered the slightest hint of negligence or misdemeanour. Never. I was an inspiration to others. I inspired the young men and women down from here and down from there. I inspired them to put their shoulders to the wheel and their noses to the grindstone and to keep faith at all costs with the structure which after all ensured the ordered government of all our lives, which took perfect care of us, which held us to its bosom, as it were. I was a first-class civil servant. I was admired and respected. I do not say I was loved. I didn't want to be loved. Love is an attribute no civil servant worth his salt would give house room to. It's redundant. An excrescence. No no, I'll tell you what I was. I was an envied and feared force in the temples of the just.

BEL

But you never swore in the office?

ANDY

I would never use obscene language in the office.
Certainly not. I kept my obscene language for the home,
where it belongs.

Pause.

Oh there's something I forgot to tell you. I bumped into
Maria the other day, the day before I was stricken. She
invited me back to her flat for a slice of plumduff. I said
to her, If you have thighs prepare to bare them now.

BEL

Yes, you always entertained a healthy lust for her.

ANDY

A *healthy* lust? Do you think so?

BEL

And she for you.

ANDY

Has that been the whisper along the white sands of the
blue Caribbean? I'm dying. Am I dying?

BEL

If you were dying you'd be dead.

ANDY

How do you work that out?

BEL

You'd be dead if you were dying.

ANDY

I sometimes think I'm married to a raving lunatic! But
I'm always prepared to look on the sunny side of things.
You mean I'll see spring again? I'll see another spring?
All the paraphernalia of flowers?

BEL

What a lovely use of language. You know, you've never
used language in such a way before. You've never said
such a thing before.

ANDY

Oh so what? I've said other things, haven't I? Plenty of
other things. All my life. All my life I've been saying
plenty of other things.

BEL

Yes, it's quite true that all your life in all your personal
and social attachments the language you employed was
mainly coarse, crude, vacuous, puerile, obscene and
brutal to a degree. Most people were ready to vomit
after no more than ten minutes in your company. But
this is not to say that beneath this vicious some would
say demented exterior there did not exist a delicate even
poetic sensibility, the sensibility of a young horse in the
golden age, in the golden past of our forefathers.

Silence.

ANDY

Anyway, admit it. You always entertained a healthy lust
for Maria yourself. And she for you. But let me make
something quite clear. I was never jealous. I was not
jealous then. Nor am I jealous now.

BEL

Why should you be jealous? She was your mistress.
Throughout the early and lovely days of our marriage.

ANDY

She must have reminded me of you.

Pause.

The past is a mist.

Pause.

Once . . . I remember this . . . once . . . a woman
walked towards me across a darkening room.

Pause.

BEL

That was me.

Pause.

ANDY

You?

Third area.
Faint light. BRIDGET.

BRIDGET

I am walking slowly in a dense jungle. But I'm not
suffocating. I can breathe. That is because I can see the
sky through the leaves.

Pause.

I'm surrounded by flowers. Hibiscus, oleander,
bougainvillea, jacaranda. The turf under my feet is soft.

Pause.

I crossed so many fierce landscapes to get here. Thorns,
stones, stinging nettles, barbed wire, skeletons of men
and women in ditches. There was no hiding there.
There was no yielding. There was no solace, no shelter.

Pause.

But here there is shelter. I can hide. I am hidden. The
flowers surround me but they don't imprison me. I am
free. Hidden but free. I'm a captive no longer. I'm lost
no longer. No one can find me or see me. I can be seen
only by eyes of the jungle, eyes in the leaves. But they
don't want to harm me.

Pause.

There is a smell of burning. A velvet odour, very deep,
an echo like a bell.

337

Pause.

No one in the world can find me.

Fred's bedroom.
FRED *and* JAKE, *sitting at a table.*

JAKE

What did you say your name was? I've made a note of it somewhere.

FRED

Macpherson.

JAKE

That's funny. I thought it was Gonzalez. I would be right in saying you were born in Tooting Common?

FRED

I came here at your urgent request. You wanted to consult me.

JAKE

Did I go that far?

FRED

When I say 'you' I don't of course mean you. I mean 'they'.

JAKE

You mean Kellaway.

338

FRED

Kellaway? I don't know Kellaway.

JAKE

You don't?

FRED

Yours was the name they gave me.

JAKE

What name was that?

FRED

Saunders.

JAKE

Oh quite.

FRED

They didn't mention Kellaway.

JAKE

When you say 'they' I take it you don't mean 'they'?

FRED

I mean a man called Sims.

JAKE

Jim Sims?

FRED

No.

JAKE

Well, if it isn't Jim Sims I can't imagine what Sims you
can possibly be talking about.

FRED

That's no skin off my nose.

JAKE

I fervently hope you're right.

JAKE *examines papers*.

Oh by the way, Manning's popping in to see you in a
few minutes.

FRED

Manning?

JAKE

Yes, just to say hello. He can't stay long. He's on his
way to Huddersfield.

FRED

Manning?

JAKE

Huddersfield, yes.

FRED

I don't know any Manning.

JAKE

I know you don't. That's why he's popping in to see you.

FRED

Now look here. I think this is getting a bit out of court.
First Kellaway, now Manning. Two men I have not only
never met but have never even heard of. I'm going to
have to take this back to my people, I'm afraid. I'll have
to get a further briefing on this.

JAKE

Oh I'm terribly sorry – of course – you must know
Manning by his other name.

FRED

What's that?

JAKE

Rawlings.

FRED

I know Rawlings.

JAKE

I had no right to call him Manning.

FRED

Not if he's the Rawlings I know.

JAKE

He is the Rawlings you know.

FRED

Well, this quite clearly brings us straight back to
Kellaway. What's Kellaway's other name?

JAKE

Saunders.

Pause.

FRED

But that's your name.

RALPH *to* JAKE *and* FRED.

RALPH

Were you keen on the game of soccer when you were
lads, you boys? Probably not. Probably thinking of
other things. Kissing girls. Foreign literature. Snooker. I
know the form. I can tell by the complexion, I can tell
by the stance, I can tell by the way a man holds himself
whether he has an outdoor disposition or not. Your
father could never be described as a natural athlete. Not
by a long chalk. The man was a thinker. Well, there's a
place in this world for thinking, I certainly wouldn't
argue with that. The trouble with so much thinking,
though, or with that which calls itself thinking, is that
it's like farting Annie Laurie down a keyhole. A waste of
your time and mine. What do you think this thinking is
pretending to do? Eh? It's pretending to make things
clear, you see, it's pretending to clarify things. But
what's it really doing? Eh? What do you think? I'll tell
you. It's confusing you, it's blinding you, it's sending the
mind into a spin, it's making you dizzy, it's making you
so dizzy that by the end of the day you don't know
whether you're on your arse or your elbow, you don't
know whether you're coming or going. I've always been
a pretty vigorous man myself. I had a seafaring

background. I was the captain of a lugger. The bosun's name was Ripper. But after years at sea I decided to give the Arts a chance generally. I had tried a bit of amateur refereeing but it didn't work out. But I had a natural talent for acting and I also played the piano and I could paint. But I should have been an architect. That's where the money is. It was your mother and father woke me up to poetry and art. They changed my life. And then of course I married my wife. A fine woman but demanding. She was looking for fibre and guts. Her eyes were black and appalling. I dropped dead at her feet. It was all go at that time. Love, football, the arts, the occasional pint. Mind you, I preferred a fruity white wine but you couldn't actually say that in those days.

Third area.
Jake (18), Fred (17), Bridget (14).
BRIDGET *and* FRED *on the floor.* JAKE *standing.*
A cassette playing.

FRED

Why can't I come?

JAKE

I've told you. There isn't room in the car.

BRIDGET

Oh take him with you.

JAKE

There's no room in the car. It's not my car. I'm just a passenger. I'm lucky to get a lift myself.

FRED

But if I can't come with you what am I going to do all night? I'll have to stay here with her.

BRIDGET

Oh God, I wish you'd take him with you. Otherwise I'll have to stay here with him.

JAKE

Well, you are related.

FRED

That's the trouble.

BRIDGET (*To* FRED)

You're related to him too.

FRED

Yes, but once I got to this gig I'd lose him. We wouldn't see each other again. He's merely a method of transport. Emotion or family allegiances don't come in to it.

BRIDGET

Oh well go with him then.

JAKE

I've told you, he can't. There isn't any room in the car. It's not my car! I haven't got a car.

FRED

That's what's so tragic about the whole business. If you had a car none of this would be taking place.

344

BRIDGET

Look, I don't want him to stay here with me, I can assure you, I actually want to be alone.

FRED

Greta Garbo! Are you going to be a film star when you grow up?

BRIDGET

Oh shut up. You know what I'm going to be.

FRED

What?

BRIDGET

A physiotherapist.

JAKE

She'll be a great physiotherapist.

FRED

She'll have to play very soothing music so that her patients won't notice their suffering.

BRIDGET

I did your neck the other day and you didn't complain.

FRED

That's true.

BRIDGET

You had a spasm and I released it.

FRED

That's true.

BRIDGET

You didn't complain then.

FRED

I'm not complaining now. I think you're wonderful. I
know you're wonderful. And I know you'll make a
wonderful physiotherapist. But I still want to get to this
gig in Amersham. That doesn't mean I don't think
you're wonderful.

BRIDGET

Oh go to Amersham, please! You don't think I need
anyone to stay with me, do you? I'm not a child.
Anyway, I'm reading this book.

JAKE

You don't want to be all on your own.

BRIDGET

I *do* want to be all on my own. I want to read this
book.

FRED

I don't even have a book. I mean – I have books – but
they're all absolutely unreadable.

JAKE

Well I'm off to Amersham.

FRED

What about me?

BRIDGET

Oh for God's sake take him with you to Amersham or don't take him with you to Amersham or shut up! Both of you!

Pause.

JAKE

Well I'm off to Amersham.

He goes. BRIDGET *and* FRED *sit still.*
Music plays.

Andy's room.
ANDY *and* BEL.

BEL

I'm giving you a mushroom omelette today and a little green salad – and an apple.

ANDY

How kind you are. I'd be lost without you. It's true. I'd flounder without you. I'd fall apart. Well, I'm falling apart as it is – but if I didn't have you I'd stand no chance.

BEL

You're not a bad man. You're just what we used to call a loudmouth. You can't help it. It's your nature. If you

347

only kept your mouth shut more of the time life with you might just be tolerable.

ANDY

Allow me to kiss your hand. I owe you everything.

He watches her embroider.

Oh, I've been meaning to ask you, what are you making there? A winding sheet? Are you going to wrap me up in it when I conk out? You'd better get a move on. I'm going fast.

Pause.

Where are they?

Pause.

Two sons. Absent. Indifferent. Their father dying.

BEL

They were good boys. I've been thinking of how they used to help me with the washing-up. And the drying. The clearing of the table, the washing-up, the drying. Do you remember?

ANDY

You mean in the twilight? The soft light falling through the kitchen window? The bell ringing for Evensong in the pub round the corner?

Pause.

348

They were bastards. Both of them. Always. Do you
remember that time I asked Jake to clean out the broom
cupboard? Well – I *told* him – I admit it – I didn't ask
him – I told him that it was bloody filthy and that he
hadn't lifted a little finger all week. Nor had the other
one. Lazy idle layabouts. Anyway all I did was to ask
him – quite politely – to clean out the bloody broom
cupboard. His defiance! Do you remember the way he
looked at me? His defiance!

Pause.

And look at them now! What are they now! A sponging
parasitical pair of ponces. Sucking the tit of the state.
Sucking the tit of the state! And I bet you feed them a
few weekly rupees from your little money-box, don't
you? Because they always loved their loving mother.
They helped her with the washing-up!

Pause.

I've got to stretch my legs. Go over the Common, watch
a game of football, rain or shine. What was the name of
that old chum of mine? Used to referee amateur games
every weekend? On the Common? Charming bloke.
They treated him like shit. A subject of scorn. No
decision he ever made was adhered to or respected.
They shouted at him, they screamed at him, they called
him every kind of prick. I used to watch in horror from
the touchline. I'll always remember his impotent
whistle. It blows down to me through the ages, damp
and forlorn. What was his name? And now I'm dying
and he's probably dead.

349

BEL

He's not dead.

ANDY

Why not?

Pause.

What was his name?

BEL

Ralph.

ANDY

Ralph? Ralph? Can that be possible?

Pause.

Well, even if his name was Ralph he was still the most sensitive and intelligent of men. My oldest friend. But pathologically idiosyncratic, if he was anything. He was reliable enough when he was sitting down but you never knew where you were with him when he was standing up, I mean when he was on the move, when you were walking down the street with him. He was a reticent man, you see. He said little but he was always thinking. And the trouble was – his stride would keep pace with his thoughts. If he was thinking slowly he'd walk as if he was wading through mud or crawling out of a pot of apricot jam. If he was thinking quickly he walked like greased lightning, you couldn't keep up with him, you were on your knees in the gutter while he

350

was over the horizon in a flash. I always had a lot of
sympathy for his sexual partner, whoever she may have
been. I mean to say – one minute he'd be berserk – up
to a thousand revolutions a second – and the next he'd
be grinding to the most appalling and deadly halt. He
was his own natural handbrake. Poor girl. There must
be easier ways of making ends meet.

Pause.

Anyway, leaving him aside, if you don't mind, for a few
minutes, where is Maria? Why isn't she here? I can't die
without her.

BEL

Oh of course you can. And you will.

ANDY

But think of our past. We were all so close. Think of the
months I betrayed you with her. How can she forget?
Think of the wonder of it. I betrayed you with your
own girlfriend, she betrayed you with your husband
and she betrayed her own husband – and me – with
you! She broke every record in sight! She was a genius
and a great fuck.

BEL

She was a very charming and attractive woman.

ANDY

Then why isn't she here? She loved me, not to mention
you. Why isn't she here to console you in your grief.

BEL

She's probably forgotten you're dying. If she ever remembered.

ANDY

What! What!

Pause.

I had her in our bedroom, by the way, once or twice, on our bed. I was a man at the time.

Pause.

You probably had her in the same place, of course. In our bedroom, on our bed.

BEL

I don't 'have' people.

ANDY

You've had me.

BEL

Oh you. Oh yes. I can still have you.

ANDY

What do you mean? Are you threatening me? What do you have in mind? Assault? Are you proposing to have me here and now? Without further ado? Would it be out of order to remind you that I'm on my deathbed? Or is that a solecism? What's your plan, to kill me in the act, like a praying mantis? How much sexual juice

352

does a corpse retain and for how long, for Christ's sake?
The truth is I'm basically innocent. I know little of
women. But I've heard dread tales. Mainly from my old
mate, the referee. But they were probably all fantasy
and fabrication, bearing no relation whatsoever to
reality.

BEL

Oh, do you think so? Do you really think so?

Fred's room.
FRED *and* JAKE, *at the table.*

JAKE

The meeting is scheduled for 6.30. Bellamy in the chair.
Pratt, Hawkeye, Belcher and Rausch, Horsfall
attending. Lieutenant-Colonel Silvio d'Orangerie will
speak off the record at 7.15 precisely.

FRED

But Horsfall *will* be attending?

JAKE

Oh, Horsfall's always steady on parade. Apart from
that I've done the placement myself.

FRED

What are you, the permanent secretary?

JAKE

Indeed I am. Indeed I am.

FRED

Funny Hawkeye and Rausch being at the same table.
Did you mention Bigsby?

JAKE

Why, did Hawkeye tangle with Rausch at Bromley? No,
I didn't mention Bigsby.

FRED

They were daggers drawn at Eastbourne.

JAKE

What, during the Buckminster hierarchy?

FRED

Buckminster? I never mentioned Buckminster.

JAKE

You mentioned Bigsby.

FRED

You're not telling me that Bigsby is anything to do with
Buckminster? Or that Buckminster and Bigsby – ?

JAKE

I'm telling you nothing of the sort. Buckminster and
Bigsby are two quite different people.

FRED

That's always been my firm conviction.

JAKE

Well, thank goodness we agree about something.

FRED

I've never thought we were all that far apart.

JAKE

You mean where it matters most?

FRED

Quite. Tell me more about Belcher.

JAKE

Belcher? Who's Belcher? Oh, Belcher! Sorry. I thought for a moment you were confusing Belcher with Bellamy. Because of the B's. You follow me?

FRED

Any confusion that exists in that area rests entirely in you, old chap.

JAKE

That's a bit blunt, isn't it? Are you always so blunt? After all, I've got a steady job here, which is more than can be said for you.

FRED

Listen son. I've come a long way down here to attend a series of highly confidential meetings in which my participation is seen to be a central factor. I've come a very long way and the people I left to man the bloody fort made quite clear to me a number of their very weighty misgivings. But I insisted and here I am. I want to see Bellamy, I want to see Belcher, I need to see Rausch, Pratt is a prat but Hawkeye is crucial. Frustrate any of this and you'll regret it.

JAKE

I can only hope Lieutenant-Colonel Silvio d'Orangerie
won't find you as offensive as I do. He's an incredibly
violent person.

FRED

I know Silvio.

JAKE

Know him? What do you mean?

FRED

We were together in Torquay.

JAKE

Oh. I see.

Pause.

What about Horsfall?

FRED

Horsfall belongs to you.

Andy's room.
ANDY *and* BEL.

ANDY

Where is she? Of all the people in the world I know
she'd want to be with me now. Because she I know
remembers everything. How I cuddled her and sang to

her, how I kept her nightmares from her, how she fell
asleep in my arms.

BEL

Please. Oh please.

Pause.

ANDY

Is she bringing my grandchildren to see me? Is she? To
catch their last look of me, to receive my blessing?

BEL *sits frozen.*

Poor little buggers, their eyes so wide, so blue, so black,
poor tots, tiny totlets, poor little tiny totlets, to lose
their grandad at the height of his powers, when he was
about to stumble upon new reserves of spiritual zest,
when the door was about to open on new ever-widening
and ever-lengthening horizons.

BEL

But darling, death will be your new horizon.

ANDY

What?

BEL

Death is your new horizon.

ANDY

That may be. That may be. But the big question is, will
I cross it as I die or after I'm dead? Or perhaps I won't

357

cross it at all. Perhaps I'll just stay stuck in the middle of
the horizon. In which case, can I see over it? Can I see
to the other side? Or is the horizon endless? And what's
the weather like? Is it uncertain with showers or sunny
with fogpatches? Or unceasing moonlight with no
cloud? Or pitch black for ever and ever? You may say
you haven't the faintest fucking idea and you would be
right. But personally I don't believe it's going to be pitch
black for ever because if it's pitch black for ever what
would have been the point of going through all these
enervating charades in the first place? There must be a
loophole. The only trouble is, I can't find it. If only I
could find it I would crawl through it and meet myself
coming back. Like screaming with fright at the sight of
a stranger only to find you're looking into a mirror.

Pause.

But what if I cross this horizon before my grandchildren
get here? They won't know where I am. What will they
say? Will you ever tell me? Will you ever tell me what
they say? They'll cry or they won't, a sorrow too deep
for tears, but they're only babies, what can they know
about death?

BEL

Oh, the really little ones I think do know something about
death, they know more about death than we do. We've
forgotten death but they haven't forgotten it. They
remember it. Because some of them, those who are really
very young, remember the moment before their life began
– it's not such a long time ago for them, you see – and the
moment before their life began they were of course dead.

Pause.

ANDY

Really?

BEL

Of course.

Half-light over the whole stage.
Stillness. A telephone rings in Fred's room. It rings six times. A click. Silence.
Blackout.

Third area.
Faint light. ANDY *moving about in the dark. He stubs his toe.*

ANDY

Shit!

He moves to an alcove.

Why not? No fags, no fucks. Bollocks to the lot of them. I'll have a slug anyway. Bollocks to the lot of them and bugger them all.

Sound of bottle opening. Pouring. He drinks, sighs.

Ah God. That's the ticket. Just the job. Bollocks to the lot of them.

359

He pours again, drinks.
Growing moonlight finds BRIDGET *in background,*
standing still.
ANDY *moves into the light and stops still, listening.*
Silence.

Ah darling. Ah my darling.

BEL *appears. She walks into moonlight.* ANDY *and* BEL
look at each other. They turn away from each other.
They stand still, listening. BRIDGET *remains still, in*
background.
Silence.
Lights fade on ANDY *and* BELL.
BRIDGET, *standing in the moonlight.*
Light fades.

Fred's room.
JAKE *and* FRED. FRED *in bed.*

JAKE
How's your water consumption these days?

FRED
I've given all that up.

JAKE
Really?

FRED
Oh yes. I've decided to eschew the path of purity and
abstention and take up a proper theology. From now on

it's the Michelin Guide and the Orient Express for me –
that kind of thing.

JAKE

I once lived the life of Riley myself.

FRED

What was he like?

JAKE

I never met him personally. But I became a very very
close friend of the woman he ran away with.

FRED

I bet she taught you a thing or two.

JAKE

She taught me nothing she hadn't learnt herself at the
feet of the master.

FRED

Wasn't Riley known under his other hat as the Sheikh
of Araby?

JAKE

That's him. His mother was one of the all-time-great
belly dancers and his father was one of the last of the
great village elders.

FRED

A marvellous people.

JAKE

A proud people too.

FRED

Watchful.

JAKE

Wary.

FRED

Touchy.

JAKE

Bristly.

FRED

Vengeful.

JAKE

Absolutely ferocious, to be quite frank.

FRED

Kick you in the balls as soon as look at you.

JAKE

But you know what made them the men they were?

FRED

What?

JAKE

They drank water. Sheer, cold, sparkling mountain water.

FRED

And this made men of them?

JAKE

And Gods.

FRED

I'll have some then. I've always wanted to be a God.

JAKE (*Pouring*)

Drink up.

FRED

Listen. Can I ask you a very personal question? Do you
think my nerve is going? Do you think my nerve is on
the blink?

JAKE

I'm going to need a second opinion.

FRED

We haven't had the first one yet.

JAKE

No, no, the second is always the one that counts, any
fool knows that. But I've got another suggestion.

FRED

What's that?

JAKE

What about a walk around the block?

FRED

Oh no, I'm much happier in bed. Staying in bed suits me. I'd be very unhappy to get out of bed and go out and meet strangers and all that kind of thing. I'd really much prefer to stay in my bed.

Pause.

Bridget would understand. I was her brother. She understood me. She always understood my feelings.

JAKE

She understood me too.

Pause.

She understood me too.

Silence.

FRED

Listen. I've got a funny feeling my equilibrium is in tatters.

JAKE

Oh really? Well they can prove these things scientifically now, you know. I beg you to remember that.

FRED

Really?

JAKE

Oh yes. They've got things like light-meters now.

FRED

Light-meters?

JAKE

Oh yes. They can test the quality of light down to a
fraction of a centimetre, even if it's pitch dark.

FRED

They can find whatever light is left in the dark?

JAKE

They can find it, yes. They can locate it. Then they place
it in a little box. They wrap it up and tie a ribbon round
it and you get it tax free, as a reward for all your labour
and faith and all the concern and care for others you
have demonstrated so eloquently for so long.

FRED

And will it serve me as a light at the end of the tunnel?

JAKE

It will serve you as a torch, as a flame. It will serve you
as your own personal light eternal.

FRED

Fantastic.

JAKE

This is what we can do for you.

FRED

Who?

JAKE

Society.

Pause.

FRED

Listen. I'd like – if you don't mind – to take you back to
the remarks you were making earlier – about your
father – and about your inheritance – which was not
perhaps quite what it purported to be, which was not,
shall we say, exactly the bona fide gold-plated testament
deep-seated rumour had reckoned but which was – in
fact – according to information we now possess – in the
lowest category of Ruritanian fantasy –

JAKE

Yes, but wait a minute! What exactly is being said here
about my Dad? What is being said? What is this? What
it demonstrably is not is a dissertation upon the
defeated or a lament for the lost, is it? No, no, I'll tell
you what it is. It is an atrociously biased and
illegitimate onslaught on the weak and vertiginous. Do
you follow me? So what is this? I am entitled to ask.
What is being said? What is being said here? What is it
that is being said here – or there – for that matter? I ask
this question. In other words, I am asking this question.
What finally is being said?

Pause.

All his life my father has been subjected to hatred and
vituperation. He has been from time immemorial
pursued and persecuted by a malignant force which

until this day has remained shadowy, a force resisting definition or classification. What is this force and what is its bent? You will answer that question, not I. You will, in the calm and ease which will come to you, as assuredly it will, in due course, before the last race is run, answer that question, not I. I will say only this: I contend that you subject to your scorn a man who was – and here I pray for your understanding – an innocent bystander to his own nausea. At the age of three that man was already at the end of his tether. No wonder he yearned to leave to his loving son the legacy of all that was best and most valuable of his life and death. He loved me. And one day I shall love him. I shall love him and be happy to pay the full price of that love.

FRED

Which is the price of death.

JAKE

The price of death, yes.

FRED

Than which there is no greater price.

JAKE

Than which?

FRED

Than which.

Pause.

Death –

367

JAKE

Which is the price of love.

FRED

A great great price.

JAKE

A great and deadly price.

FRED

But strictly in accordance with the will of God.

JAKE

And the laws of nature.

FRED

And common or garden astrological logic.

JAKE

It's the first axiom.

FRED

And the last.

JAKE

It may well be both tautologous and contradictory.

FRED

But it nevertheless constitutes a watertight philosophical proposition which will in the final reckoning be seen to be such.

JAKE

I believe that to be so, yes. I believe that to be the case
and I'd like to raise a glass to all those we left behind, to
all those who fell at the first and all consequent hurdles.

They raise glasses.

FRED

Raising.

JAKE

Raising.

They drink.

FRED

Let me say this. I knew your father.

JAKE

You did indeed.

FRED

I was close to him.

JAKE

You were indeed.

FRED

Closer to him than you were yourself perhaps.

JAKE

It could be argued so. You were indeed his youngest and
most favoured son.

FRED

Precisely. And so let me say this. He was a man, take him for all in all, I shall not look upon his like again.

JAKE

You move me much.

Pause.

FRED

Some say of course that he was spiritually furtive, politically bankrupt, morally scabrous and intellectually abject.

Pause.

JAKE

They lie.

FRED

Certainly he liked a drink.

JAKE

And could be spasmodically rampant.

FRED

On my oath, there's many a maiden will attest to that.

JAKE

He may have been poetically downtrodden –

FRED

But while steeped in introversion he remained proud and fiery.

JAKE

And still I called him Dad.

Pause.

FRED

What was he like in real life? Would you say?

JAKE

A leader of men.

Pause.

FRED

What was the celebrated nickname attached to him by his friends with affection, awe and admiration?

JAKE

The Incumbent. Be at the Black Horse tonight 7.30 sharp. The Incumbent'll be there in his corner, buying a few pints for the lads.

FRED

They were behind him to a man.

JAKE

He knew his beer and possessed the classic formula for dealing with troublemakers.

FRED

What was that?

JAKE

A butcher's hook.

Pause.

FRED

Tell me about your mother.

JAKE

Don't talk dirty to me.

Andy's room.
ANDY *and* BEL.

BEL

The first time Maria and I had lunch together – in a
restaurant – I asked her to order for me. She wore grey.
A grey dress. I said please order for me, please, I'll have
whatever you decide, I'd much prefer that. And she
took my hand and squeezed it and smiled and ordered
for me.

ANDY

I saw her do it. I saw her, I heard her order for you.

BEL

I said, I'll be really happy to have whatever you decide.

ANDY

Fish. She decided on fish.

BEL

She asked about my girlhood.

372

ANDY

The bitch.

BEL

I spoke to her in a way I had never spoken to anyone
before. I told her of my girlhood. I told her about
running on the cliffs with my brothers, I ran so fast, up
and down the heather, I was so out of breath, I had to
stop, I fell down on the heather, bouncing, they fell
down at my side, and all the wind. I told her about the
wind and my brothers running after me on the clifftop
and falling down at my side.

Pause.

I spoke to her in a way I had never spoken to anyone
before. Sometimes it happens, doesn't it? You're
speaking to someone and you suddenly find that you're
another person.

ANDY

Who is?

BEL

You are.

Pause.

I don't mean you. I mean me.

ANDY

I witnessed all this, by the way.

BEL

Oh, were you there?

ANDY

I was spying on you both from a corner table, behind a vase of flowers and *The Brothers Karamazov*.

BEL

And then she said women had something men didn't have. They had certain qualities men simply didn't have. I wondered if she was talking about me. But then I realised of course she was talking about women in general. But then she looked at me and she said. You, for example. But I said to myself, Men can be beautiful too.

ANDY

I was there. I heard every word.

BEL

Not my thoughts.

ANDY

I heard your thoughts. I could hear your thoughts. You thought to yourself, Men can be beautiful too. But you didn't dare say it. But you did dare think it.

Pause.

Mind you, she thought the same. I know she did.

Pause.

374

She's the one we both should have married.

BEL

Oh no, I don't think so. I think I should have married
your friend Ralph.

ANDY

Ralph? What, Ralph the referee?

BEL

Yes.

ANDY

But he was such a terrible referee! He was such a
hopeless referee!

BEL

It wasn't the referee I loved.

ANDY

It was the man!

Pause.

Well, I'll be buggered. It's wonderful. Here I am dying
and she tells me she loved a referee. I could puke.

Pause.

And how I loved you. I'll never forget the earliest and
loveliest days of our marriage. You offered your body
to me. Here you are, you said one day, here's my body.
Oh thanks very much, I said, that's very decent of you,

375

what do you want me to do with it? Do what you will, you said. This is going to need a bit of thought, I said. I tell you what, hold on to it for a couple of minutes, will you? Hold on to it while I call a copper.

BEL

Ralph had such beautiful manners and such a lovely singing voice. I've never understood why he didn't become a professional tenor. But I think all the travel involved in that kind of life was the problem. There was a story about an old mother, a bewildered aunt. Something that tugged at his heart. I never quite knew what to believe.

ANDY

No, no, you've got the wrong bloke. My Ralph was pedantic and scholastic. Never missed a day at night school. Big ears but little feet. Never smiled. One day though he did say something. He pulled me into a doorway. He whispered in my ear. Do you know what he said? He said men had something women simply didn't have. I asked him what it was. But of course there was no way he was going to answer that question. You know why? Because referees are not obliged to answer questions. Referees are the law. They are law in action. They have a whistle. They blow it. And that whistle is the articulation of God's justice.

MARIA *and* RALPH *to* ANDY *and* BEL.

MARIA

How wonderful you both look. It's been ages. We don't live up here any more, of course.

376

RALPH

Got a place in the country.

MARIA

Years ago.

RALPH

Ten. Ten years ago.

MARIA

We've made friends with so many cows, haven't we, darling? Sarah's doing marvellously well and Lucien's thriving at the Consulate and as for Susannah, there's no stopping her. They all take after Ralph. Don't they darling? I mean physically. Mentally and artistically they take after me. We have a pretty rundown sort of quite large cottage. Not exactly a château. A small lake.

RALPH

More of a pond.

MARIA

More of a lake, I'd say.

ANDY

So you've given up refereeing?

RALPH

Oh yes. I gave that up. And I've never regretted it.

ANDY

You mean it didn't come from the heart?

RALPH

I wasn't born for it.

ANDY

Well, you were certainly no bloody good at it.

Pause.

RALPH

Tell me. I often think of the past. Do you?

ANDY

The past? What past? I don't remember any past. What kind of past did you have in mind?

RALPH

Walking down the Balls Pond Road, for example.

ANDY

I never went anywhere near the Balls Pond Road. I was a civil servant. I had no past. I remember no past. Nothing ever happened.

BEL

Yes it did.

MARIA

Oh it did. Yes it did. Lots of things happened.

RALPH

Yes, things happened. Things certainly happened. All sorts of things happened.

BEL

All sorts of things happened.

ANDY

Well, I don't remember any of these things. I remember none of these things.

MARIA

For instance, your children! Your lovely little girl! Bridget! (*She laughs.*) Little girl! She must be a mother by now.

Pause.

ANDY

I've got three beautiful grandchildren. (*To* BEL) Haven't I?

Pause.

BEL

By the way, he's not well. Have you noticed?

RALPH

Who?

BEL

Him.

MARIA

I hadn't noticed.

RALPH

What's the trouble?

BEL

He's on the way out.

Pause.

RALPH

Old Andy? Not a chance. He was always as fit as a
fiddle. Constitution like an ox.

MARIA

People like Andy never die. That's the wonderful thing
about them.

RALPH

He looks in the pink.

MARIA

A bit peaky perhaps but in the pink. He'll be running
along the towpath in next to no time. Take my word.
Waltzing away in next to no time.

RALPH

Before you can say Jack Robinson. Well, we must
toddle.

RALPH *and* MARIA *out.*
BEL *goes to telephone, dials.*
Lights hold on her.

Lights up in Fred's room.
The phone rings. JAKE *picks it up.*

JAKE

Chinese laundry?

BEL

Your father is very ill.

JAKE

Chinese laundry?

Silence.

BEL

Your father is very ill.

JAKE

Can I pass you to my colleague?

FRED *takes the phone.*

FRED

Chinese laundry?

Pause.

BEL

It doesn't matter.

FRED

Oh my dear madam, absolutely everything matters
when it comes down to laundry.

BEL

No. It doesn't matter. It doesn't matter.

Silence.
JAKE *takes the phone, looks at it, puts it to his ear.*
BEL *holds the phone.*
FRED *grabs the phone.*

FRED

If you have any serious complaint can we refer you to
our head office?

BEL

Do you do dry cleaning?

FRED *is still. He then passes the phone to* JAKE.

JAKE

Hullo. Can I help you?

BEL

Do you do dry cleaning?

JAKE *is still.*
BEL *puts the phone down. Dialling tone.*
JAKE *replaces phone.*

JAKE

Of course we do dry cleaning! Of course we do dry
cleaning! What kind of fucking laundry are you if you
don't do dry cleaning?

Andy's room.
ANDY *and* BEL.

ANDY

Where are they? My grandchildren? The babies? My
daughter?

Pause.

Are they waiting outside? Why do you keep them
waiting outside? Why can't they come in? What are
they waiting for?

Pause.

What's happening

Pause.

What is happening?

BEL

Are you dying?

ANDY

Am I?

BEL

Don't you know?

ANDY

No, I don't know. I don't know how it feels. How does
it feel?

ANDY

BEL

I don't know.

Pause.

ANDY

Why don't they come in? Are they frightened? Tell them not to be frightened.

BEL

They're not here. They haven't come.

ANDY

Tell Bridget not to be frightened. Tell Bridget I don't want her to be frightened.

Fred's room.
JAKE *and* FRED.
FRED *is out of bed. He wears shorts. They both walk around the room, hands behind backs.*

JAKE

Pity you weren't at d'Orangerie's memorial.

FRED

I'm afraid I was confined to my bed with a mortal disease.

JAKE

So I gather. Pity. It was a great do.

FRED

Was it?

JAKE

Oh yes. Everyone was there.

FRED

Really? Who?

JAKE

Oh . . . Denton, Alabaster, Tunnicliffe, Quinn.

FRED

Really?

JAKE

Oh yes. Kelly, Mortlake, Longman, Small.

FRED

Good Lord.

JAKE

Oh yes. Wetterby, White, Hotchkiss, De Groot . . .
Blackhouse, Garland, Gupte, Tate.

FRED

Well, well!

JAKE

The whole gang. Donovan, Ironside, Wallace, McCool
. . . Ottuna, Muggeridge, Carpentier, Finn.

FRED

Speeches?

JAKE

Very moving.

FRED

Who spoke?

JAKE

Oh . . . Hazeldine, McCormick, Bugatti, Black, Forrester, Galloway, Springfield, Gaunt.

FRED

He was much loved.

JAKE

Well, you loved him yourself, didn't you?

FRED

I loved him. I loved him like a father.

Third area.

BRIDGET

Once someone said to me – I think it was my mother or my father – anyway, they said to me – We've been invited to a party. You've been invited too. But you'll have to come by yourself, alone. You won't have to dress up. You just have to wait until the moon is down.

Pause.

They told me where the party was. It was in a house at
the end of a lane. But they told me the party wouldn't
begin until the moon had gone down.

Pause.

I got dressed in something old and I waited for the
moon to go down. I waited a long time. Then I set out
for the house. The moon was bright and quite still.

Pause.

When I got to the house it was bathed in moonlight.
The house, the glade, the lane, were all bathed in
moonlight. But the inside of the house was dark and all
the windows were dark. There was no sound.

Pause.

I stood there in the moonlight and waited for the moon
to go down.

ASHES TO ASHES

Ashes to Ashes was first presented by the Royal Court at the Ambassadors Theatre, London, on 12 September 1996. The cast was as follows:

DEVLIN   Stephen Rea
REBECCA   Lindsay Duncan

Directed by Harold Pinter
Designed by Eileen Diss
Lighting by Mick Hughes
Costume by Tom Rand
Sound by Tom Lishman

A house in the country.

Ground-floor room. A large window.
Garden beyond.

Two armchairs. Two lamps.

Early evening. Summer.

The room darkens during the course of the play.
The lamplight intensifies.

By the end of the play the room and the garden beyond
are only dimly defined.
The lamplight has become very bright but does not
illumine the room.

DEVLIN *standing with drink.* REBECCA *sitting.*

Silence.

REBECCA
Well . . . for example . . . he would stand over me and clench his fist. And then he'd put his other hand on my neck and grip it and bring my head towards him. His fist . . . grazed my mouth. And he'd say, 'Kiss my fist.'

DEVLIN
And did you?

REBECCA
Oh yes. I kissed his fist. The knuckles. And then he'd open his hand and give me the palm of his hand . . . to kiss . . . which I kissed.

Pause.

And then I would speak.

DEVLIN
What did you say? You said what? What did you say?

Pause.

REBECCA

I said, 'Put your hand round my throat.' I murmured it through his hand, as I was kissing it, but he heard my voice, he heard it through his hand, he felt my voice in his hand, he heard it there.

Silence.

DEVLIN

And did he? Did he put his hand round your throat?

REBECCA

Oh yes. He did. He did. And he held it there, very gently, very gently, so gently. He adored me, you see.

DEVLIN

He adored you?

Pause.

What do you mean, he adored you? What do you mean?

Pause.

Are you saying he put no pressure on your throat? Is that what you're saying?

REBECCA

No.

DEVLIN

What then? What are you saying?

REBECCA

He put a little . . . pressure . . . on my throat, yes. So
that my head started to go back, gently but truly.

DEVLIN

And your body? Where did your body go?

REBECCA

My body went back, slowly but truly.

DEVLIN

So your legs were opening?

REBECCA

Yes.

Pause.

DEVLIN

Your legs were opening?

REBECCA

Yes.

Silence.

DEVLIN

Do you feel you're being hypnotised?

REBECCA

When?

DEVLIN

Now.

REBECCA

No.

DEVLIN

Really?

REBECCA

No.

DEVLIN

Why not?

REBECCA

Who by?

DEVLIN

By me.

REBECCA

You?

DEVLIN

What do you think?

REBECCA

I think you're a fuckpig.

DEVLIN

Me a fuckpig? Me! You must be joking.

REBECCA *smiles*.

REBECCA
Me joking? You must be joking.

Pause.

DEVLIN
You understand why I'm asking you these questions.
Don't you? Put yourself in my place. I'm compelled to
ask you questions. There are so many things I don't
know. I know nothing . . . about any of this. Nothing.
I'm in the dark. I need light. Or do you think my
questions are illegitimate?

Pause.

REBECCA
What questions?

Pause.

DEVLIN
Look. It would mean a great deal to me if you could
define him more clearly.

REBECCA
Define him? What do you mean, define him?

DEVLIN
Physically. I mean, what did he actually look like? If
you see what I mean? Length, breadth . . . that sort of
thing. Height, width. I mean, quite apart from his . . .

399

disposition, whatever that may have been . . . or his
character . . . or his spiritual . . . standing . . . I just
want, well, I need . . . to have a clearer idea of him . . .
well, not a clearer idea . . . just an idea, in fact . . .
because I have absolutely no idea . . . as things stand
. . . of what he looked like.
I mean, what did he *look like*? Can't you give him a
shape for me, a concrete shape? I want a concrete image
of him, you see . . . an image I can carry about with me.
I mean, all you can talk of are his hands, one hand over
your face, the other on the back of your neck, then the
first one on your throat. There must be more to him
than hands. What about eyes? Did he have any eyes?

REBECCA

What colour?

Pause.

DEVLIN

That's precisely the question I'm asking you . . . my
darling.

REBECCA

How odd to be called darling. No one has ever called
me darling. Apart from my lover.

DEVLIN

I don't believe it.

REBECCA

You don't believe what?

DEVLIN

I don't believe he ever called you darling.

Pause.

Do you think my use of the word is illegitimate?

REBECCA

What word?

DEVLIN

Darling.

REBECCA

Oh yes, you called me darling. How funny.

DEVLIN

Funny? Why?

REBECCA

Well, how can you possibly call me darling? I'm not your darling.

DEVLIN

Yes you are.

REBECCA

Well I don't want to be your darling. It's the last thing I want to be. I'm nobody's darling.

DEVLIN

That's a song.

REBECCA

What?

DEVLIN

'I'm nobody's baby now'.

REBECCA

It's '*You're* nobody's baby now'. But anyway, I didn't use the word baby.

Pause.

I can't tell you what he looked like.

DEVLIN

Have you forgotten?

REBECCA

No. I haven't forgotten. But that's not the point. Anyway, he went away years ago.

DEVLIN

Went away? Where did he go?

REBECCA

His job took him away. He had a job.

DEVLIN

What was it?

REBECCA

What?

DEVLIN

What kind of job was it? What job?

REBECCA

I think it had something to do with a travel agency. I
think he was some kind of courier. No. No, he wasn't.
That was only a part-time job. I mean that was only
part of the job in the agency. He was quite high up, you
see. He had a lot of responsibilities.

Pause.

DEVLIN

What sort of agency?

REBECCA

A travel agency.

DEVLIN

What sort of travel agency?

REBECCA

He was a guide, you see. A guide.

DEVLIN

A tourist guide?

Pause.

REBECCA

Did I ever tell you about that place . . . about the time
he took me to that place?

403

DEVLIN

What place?

REBECCA

I'm sure I told you.

DEVLIN

No. You never told me.

REBECCA

How funny. I could swear I had. Told you.

DEVLIN

You haven't told me anything. You've never spoken about him before. You haven't told me anything.

Pause.

What place?

REBECCA

Oh, it was a kind of factory, I suppose.

DEVLIN

What do you mean, a kind of factory? Was it a factory or wasn't it? And if it was a factory, what kind of factory was it?

REBECCA

Well, they were making things – just like any other factory. But it wasn't the usual kind of factory.

DEVLIN

Why not?

REBECCA

They were all wearing caps . . . the workpeople . . . soft
caps . . . and they took them off when he came in,
leading me, when he led me down the alleys between
the rows of workpeople.

DEVLIN

They took their caps off? You mean they doffed them?

REBECCA

Yes.

DEVLIN

Why did they do that?

REBECCA

He told me afterwards it was because they had such
great respect for him.

DEVLIN

Why?

REBECCA

Because he ran a really tight ship, he said. They had
total faith in him. They respected his . . . purity, his . . .
conviction. They would follow him over a cliff and into
the sea, if he asked them, he said. And sing in a chorus,
as long as he led them. They were in fact very musical,
he said.

DEVLIN

What did they make of you?

REBECCA

Me? Oh, they were sweet. I smiled at them. And
immediately every single one of them smiled back.

Pause.

The only thing was – the place was so damp. It was
exceedingly damp.

DEVLIN

And they weren't dressed for the weather?

REBECCA

No.

Pause.

DEVLIN

I thought you said he worked for a travel agency?

REBECCA

And there was one other thing. I wanted to go to the
bathroom. But I simply couldn't find it. I looked
everywhere. I'm sure they had one. But I never found
out where it was.

Pause.

He did work for a travel agency. He was a guide. He
used to go to the local railway station and walk down

406

the platform and tear all the babies from the arms of
their screaming mothers.

Pause.

DEVLIN

Did he?

Silence.

REBECCA

By the way, I'm terribly upset.

DEVLIN

Are you? Why?

REBECCA

Well, it's about that police siren we heard a couple of
minutes ago.

DEVLIN

What police siren?

REBECCA

Didn't you hear it? You must have heard it. Just a
couple of minutes ago.

DEVLIN

What about it?

REBECCA

Well, I'm just terribly upset.

407

Pause.

I'm just incredibly upset.

Pause.

Don't you want to know why? Well, I'm going to tell you anyway. If I can't tell you who can I tell? Well, I'll tell you anyway. It just hit me so hard. You see . . . as the siren faded away in my ears I knew it was becoming louder and louder for somebody else.

DEVLIN
You mean that it's always being heard by somebody, somewhere? Is that what you're saying?

REBECCA
Yes. Always. For ever.

DEVLIN
Does that make you feel secure?

REBECCA
No! It makes me feel insecure! Terribly insecure.

DEVLIN
Why?

REBECCA
I hate it fading away. I hate it echoing away. I hate it leaving me. I hate losing it. I hate somebody else possessing it. I want it to be mine, all the time. It's such a beautiful sound. Don't you think?

408

DEVLIN

Don't worry, there'll always be another one. There's one
on its way to you now. Believe me. You'll hear it again
soon. Any minute.

REBECCA

Will I?

DEVLIN

Sure. They're very busy people, the police. There's so
much for them to do. They've got so much to take care
of, to keep their eye on. They keep getting signals,
mostly in code. There isn't one minute of the day when
they're not charging around one corner or another in
the world, in their police cars, ringing their sirens. So
you can take comfort from that, at least. Can't you?
You'll never be lonely again. You'll never be without a
police siren. I promise you.

Pause.

Listen. This chap you were just talking about . . . I
mean this chap you and I have been talking about . . .
in a manner of speaking . . . when exactly did you meet
him? I mean when did all this happen exactly? I haven't
. . . how can I put this . . . quite got it into focus. Was it
before you knew me or after you knew me? That's a
question of some importance. I'm sure you'll appreciate
that.

REBECCA

By the way, there's something I've been dying to tell
you.

409

DEVLIN

What?

REBECCA

It was when I was writing a note, a few notes for the
laundry. Well . . . to put it bluntly . . . a laundry list.
Well, I put my pen on that little coffee table and it rolled
off.

DEVLIN

No?

REBECCA

It rolled right off, onto the carpet. In front of my eyes.

DEVLIN

Good God.

REBECCA

This pen, this perfectly innocent pen.

DEVLIN

You can't know it was innocent.

REBECCA

Why not?

DEVLIN

Because you don't know where it had been. You don't
know how many other hands have held it, how many
other hands have written with it, what other people
have been doing with it. You know nothing of its
history. You know nothing of its parents' history.

REBECCA

A pen has no parents.

Pause.

DEVLIN

You can't sit there and say things like that.

REBECCA

I can sit here.

DEVLIN

You can't sit there and say things like that.

REBECCA

You don't believe I'm entitled to sit here? You don't think I'm entitled to sit in this chair, in the place where I live?

DEVLIN

I'm saying that you're not entitled to sit in that chair or in or on any other chair and say things like that and it doesn't matter whether you live here or not.

REBECCA

I'm not entitled to say things like what?

DEVLIN

That that pen was innocent.

REBECCA

You think it was guilty?

Silence.

DEVLIN

I'm letting you off the hook. Have you noticed? I'm letting you slip. Or perhaps it's me who's slipping. It's dangerous. Do you notice? I'm in a quicksand.

REBECCA

Like God.

DEVLIN

God? God? You think God is sinking into a quicksand? That's what I would call a truly disgusting perception. If it can be dignified by the word perception. Be careful how you talk about God. He's the only God we have. If you let him go he won't come back. He won't even look back over his shoulder. And then what will you do? You know what it'll be like, such a vacuum? It'll be like England playing Brazil at Wembley and not a soul in the stadium. Can you imagine? Playing both halves to a totally empty house. The game of the century. Absolute silence. Not a soul watching. Absolute silence. Apart from the referee's whistle and a fair bit of fucking and blinding. If you turn away from God it means that the great and noble game of soccer will fall into permanent oblivion. No score for extra time after extra time after extra time, no score for time everlasting, for time without end. Absence. Stalemate. Paralysis. A world without a winner.

Pause.

I hope you get the picture.

Pause.

Now let me say this. A little while ago you made . . .
shall we say . . . you made a somewhat oblique
reference to your bloke . . . your lover? . . . and babies
and mothers, et cetera. And platforms. I inferred from
this that you were talking about some kind of atrocity.
Now let me ask you this. What authority do you think
you yourself possess which would give you the right to
discuss such an atrocity?

REBECCA

I have no such authority. Nothing has ever happened to
me. Nothing has ever happened to any of my friends. I
have never suffered. Nor have my friends.

DEVLIN

Good.

Pause.

Shall we talk more intimately? Let's talk about more
intimate things, let's talk about something more
personal, about something within your own immediate
experience. I mean, for example, when the hairdresser
takes your head in his hands and starts to wash your
hair very gently and to massage your scalp, when he
does that, when your eyes are closed and he does that,
he has your entire trust, doesn't he? It's not just your
head which is in his hands, is it, it's your life, it's your
spiritual . . . welfare.

Pause.

So you see what I wanted to know was this . . . when your lover had his hand on your throat, did he remind you of your hairdresser?

Pause.

I'm talking about your lover. The man who tried to murder you.

REBECCA

Murder me?

DEVLIN

Do you to death.

REBECCA

No, no. He didn't try to murder me. He didn't want to murder me.

DEVLIN

He suffocated you and strangled you. As near as makes no difference. According to your account. Didn't he?

REBECCA

No, no. He felt compassion for me. He adored me.

Pause.

DEVLIN

Did he have a name, this chap? Was he a foreigner? And where was I at the time? What do you want me to understand? Were you unfaithful to me? Why didn't you confide in me? Why didn't you confess? You would have

414

felt so much better. Honestly. You could have treated me
like a priest. You could have put me on my mettle. I've
always wanted to be put on my mettle. It used to be one
of my lifetime ambitions. Now I've missed my big
chance. Unless all this happened before I met you. In
which case you have no obligation to tell me anything.
Your past is not my business. I wouldn't dream of telling
you about my past. Not that I had one. When you lead a
life of scholarship you can't be bothered with the
humorous realities, you know, tits, that kind of thing.
Your mind is on other things, have you got an attentive
landlady, can she come up with bacon and eggs after
eleven o'clock at night, is the bed warm, does the sun rise
in the right direction, is the soup cold? Only once in a
blue moon do you wobble the chambermaid's bottom,
on the assumption there is one – chambermaid not
bottom – but of course none of this applies when you
have a wife. When you have a wife you let thought, ideas
and reflection take their course. Which means you never
let the best man win. Fuck the best man, that's always
been my motto. It's the man who ducks his head and
moves on through no matter what wind or weather who
gets there in the end. A man with guts and application.

Pause.

A man who doesn't give a shit.
A man with a rigid sense of duty.

Pause.

There's no contradiction between those last two
statements. Believe me.

Pause.

Do you follow the drift of my argument?

REBECCA
Oh yes, there's something I've forgotten to tell you. It was funny. I looked out of the garden window, out of the window into the garden, in the middle of summer, in that house in Dorset, do you remember? Oh no, you weren't there. I don't think anyone else was there. No. I was all by myself. I was alone. I was looking out of the window and I saw a whole crowd of people walking through the woods, on their way to the sea, in the direction of the sea. They seemed to be very cold, they were wearing coats, although it was such a beautiful day. A beautiful, warm, Dorset day. They were carrying bags. There were . . . guides . . . ushering them, guiding them along. They walked through the woods and I could see them in the distance walking across the cliff and down to the sea. Then I lost sight of them. I was really quite curious so I went upstairs to the highest window in the house and I looked way over the top of the treetops and I could see down to the beach. The guides . . . were ushering all these people across the beach. It was such a lovely day. It was so still and the sun was shining. And I saw all these people walk into the sea. The tide covered them slowly. Their bags bobbed about in the waves.

DEVLIN
When was that? When did you live in Dorset? I've never lived in Dorset.

Pause.

REBECCA

Oh by the way somebody told me the other day that there's a condition known as mental elephantiasis.

DEVLIN

What do you mean, 'somebody told you'? What do you mean, 'the other day'? What are you talking about?

REBECCA

This mental elephantiasis means that when you spill an ounce of gravy, for example, it immediately expands and becomes a vast sea of gravy. It becomes a sea of gravy which surrounds you on all sides and you suffocate in a voluminous sea of gravy. It's terrible. But it's all your own fault. You brought it upon yourself. You are not the *victim* of it, you are the *cause* of it. Because it was you who spilt the gravy in the first place, it was you who handed over the bundle.

Pause.

DEVLIN

The what?

REBECCA

The bundle.

Pause.

DEVLIN

So what's the question? Are you prepared to drown in

417

your own gravy? Or are you prepared to die for your country? Look. What do you say, sweetheart? Why don't we go out and drive into town and take in a movie?

REBECCA

That's funny, somewhere in a dream . . . a long time ago . . . I heard someone calling me sweetheart.

Pause.

I looked up. I'd been dreaming. I don't know whether I looked up in the dream or as I opened my eyes. But in this dream a voice was calling. That I'm certain of. This voice was calling me. It was calling me sweetheart.

Pause.

Yes.

Pause.

I walked out into the frozen city. Even the mud was frozen. And the snow was a funny colour. It wasn't white. Well, it was white but there were other colours in it. It was as if there were veins running through it. And it wasn't smooth, as snow is, as snow should be. It was bumpy. And when I got to the railway station I saw the train. Other people were there.

Pause.

And my best friend, the man I had given my heart to,

418

the man I knew was the man for me the moment we met, my dear, my most precious companion, I watched him walk down the platform and tear all the babies from the arms of their screaming mothers.

Silence.

DEVLIN

Did you see Kim and the kids?

She looks at him.

You were going to see Kim and the kids today.

She stares at him.

Your sister Kim and the kids.

REBECCA

Oh, Kim! And the kids, yes. Yes. Yes, of course I saw them. I had tea with them. Didn't I tell you?

DEVLIN

No.

REBECCA

Of course I saw them.

Pause.

DEVLIN

How were they?

419

REBECCA

Ben's talking.

DEVLIN

Really? What's he saying?

REBECCA

Oh, things like 'My name is Ben'. Things like that. And 'Mummy's name is Mummy'. Things like that.

DEVLIN

What about Betsy?

REBECCA

She's crawling.

DEVLIN

No, really?

REBECCA

I think she'll be walking before we know where we are. Honestly.

DEVLIN

Probably talking too. Saying things like 'My name is Betsy'.

REBECCA

Yes, of course I saw them. I had tea with them. But oh
. . . my poor sister . . . she doesn't know what to do.

DEVLIN

What do you mean?

REBECCA

Well, he wants to come back . . . you know . . . he keeps phoning and asking her to take him back. He says he can't bear it, he says he's given the other one up, he says he's living quite alone, he's given the other one up.

DEVLIN

Has he?

REBECCA

He says he has. He says he misses the kids.

Pause.

DEVLIN

Does he miss his wife?

REBECCA

He says he's given the other one up. He says it was never serious, you know, it was only sex.

DEVLIN

Ah.

Pause.

And Kim?

Pause.

And Kim?

REBECCA

She'll never have him back. Never. She says she'll never share a bed with him again. Never. Ever.

DEVLIN

Why not?

REBECCA

Never ever.

DEVLIN

But why not?

REBECCA

Of course I saw Kim and the kids. I had tea with them. Why did you ask? Did you think I didn't see them?

DEVLIN

No. I didn't know. It's just that you said you were going to have tea with them.

REBECCA

Well, I did have tea with them! Why shouldn't I? She's my sister.

Pause.

Guess where I went after tea? To the cinema. I saw a film.

DEVLIN

Oh? What?

REBECCA

A comedy.

DEVLIN

Uh-huh? Was it funny? Did you laugh?

REBECCA

Other people laughed. Other members of the audience.
It was funny.

DEVLIN

But you didn't laugh?

REBECCA

Other people did. It was a comedy. There was a girl . . .
you know . . . and a man. They were having lunch in a
smart New York restaurant. He made her smile.

DEVLIN

How?

REBECCA

Well . . . he told her jokes.

DEVLIN

Oh, I see.

REBECCA

And then in the next scene he took her on an expedition
to the desert, in a caravan. She'd never lived in a desert
before, you see. She had to learn how to do it.

Pause.

DEVLIN

Sounds very funny.

REBECCA

But there was a man sitting in front of me, to my right. He was absolutely still throughout the whole film. He never moved, he was rigid, like a body with rigor mortis, he never laughed once, he just sat like a corpse. I moved far away from him, I moved as far away from him as I possibly could.

Silence.

DEVLIN

Now look, let's start again. We live here. You don't live . . . in Dorset . . . or *anywhere else*. You live here with me. This is our house. You have a very nice sister. She lives close to you. She has two lovely kids. You're their aunt. You like that.

Pause.

You have a wonderful garden. You love your garden. You created it all by yourself. You have truly green fingers. You also have beautiful fingers.

Pause.

Did you hear what I said? I've just paid you a compliment. In fact I've just paid you a number of compliments. Let's start again.

REBECCA

I don't think we can start again. We started . . . a long time ago. We started. We can't start *again*. We can end again.

DEVLIN

But we've never ended.

REBECCA

Oh, we have. Again and again and again. And we can end again. And again and again. And again.

DEVLIN

Aren't you misusing the word 'end'? End means end. You can't end 'again'. You can only end once.

REBECCA

No. You can end once and then you can end again.

Silence.

(*singing softly*) 'Ashes to ashes' –

DEVLIN

'And dust to dust' –

REBECCA

'If the women don't get you' –

DEVLIN

'The liquor must.'

Pause.

425

I always knew you loved me.

REBECCA

Why?

DEVLIN

Because we like the same tunes.

Silence.

Listen.

Pause.

Why have you never told me about this lover of yours
before this? I have the right to be very angry indeed. Do
you realise that? I have the right to be very angry
indeed. Do you understand that?

Silence.

REBECCA

Oh by the way there's something I meant to tell you. I
was standing in a room at the top of a very tall
building in the middle of town. The sky was full of
stars. I was about to close the curtains but I stayed at
the window for a time looking up at the stars. Then I
looked down. I saw an old man and a little boy
walking down the street. They were both dragging
suitcases. The little boy's suitcase was bigger than he
was. It was a very bright night. Because of the stars.
The old man and the little boy were walking down the
street. They were holding each other's free hand. I

426

wondered where they were going. Anyway, I was about to close the curtains but then I suddenly saw a woman following them, carrying a baby in her arms.

Pause.

Did I tell you the street was icy? It was icy. So she had to tread very carefully. Over the bumps. The stars were out. She followed the man and the boy until they turned the corner and were gone.

Pause.

She stood still. She kissed her baby. The baby was a girl.

Pause.

She kissed her.

Pause.

She listened to the baby's heartbeat. The baby's heart was beating.

The light in the room has darkened. The lamps are very bright.

REBECCA *sits very still.*

The baby was breathing.

Pause.

427

I held her to me. She was breathing. Her heart was
beating.

DEVLIN *goes to her. He stands over her and looks
down at her.*
*He clenches his fist and holds it in front of her face. He
puts his left hand behind her neck and grips it. He
brings her head towards his fist. His fist touches her
mouth.*

DEVLIN

Kiss my fist.

She does not move.

*He opens his hand and places the palm of his hand on
her mouth.*

She does not move.

DEVLIN

Speak. Say it. Say 'Put your hand round my throat.'

She does not speak.

Ask me to put my hand round your throat.

She does not speak or move.

*He puts his hand on her throat. He presses gently. Her
head goes back.*

They are still.

428

She speaks. There is an echo. His grip loosens.

REBECCA

They took us to the trains

ECHO

the trains

He takes his hand from her throat.

REBECCA

They were taking the babies away

ECHO

the babies away

Pause.

REBECCA

I took my baby and wrapped it in my shawl

ECHO

my shawl

REBECCA

And I made it into a bundle

ECHO

a bundle

REBECCA

And I held it under my left arm

ECHO

my left arm

Pause.

REBECCA

And I went through with my baby

ECHO

my baby

Pause.

REBECCA

But the baby cried out

ECHO

cried out

REBECCA

And the man called me back

ECHO

called me back

REBECCA

And he said what do you have there

ECHO

have there

REBECCA

He stretched out his hand for the bundle

ECHO

for the bundle

REBECCA

And I gave him the bundle

ECHO

the bundle

REBECCA

And that's the last time I held the bundle

ECHO

the bundle

Silence.

REBECCA

And we got on the train

ECHO

the train

REBECCA

And we arrived at this place

ECHO

this place

REBECCA

And I met a woman I knew

ECHO

I knew

REBECCA

And she said what happened to your baby

ECHO

your baby

REBECCA

Where is your baby

ECHO

your baby

REBECCA

And I said what baby

ECHO

what baby

REBECCA

I don't have a baby

ECHO

a baby

REBECCA

I don't know of any baby

ECHO

of any baby

Pause.

REBECCA

I don't know of any baby

Long silence.

Blackout.

CELEBRATION

CHARACTERS

LAMBERT
MATT
PRUE
JULIE
RUSSELL
SUKI
RICHARD
SONIA
WAITER
WAITRESS 1
WAITRESS 2

A restaurant.

Two curved banquettes.

Celebration was first presented in a double bill with *The Room* at the Almeida Theatre, London, on 16 March 2000, with the following cast:

LAMBERT	Keith Allen
MATT	Andy de la Tour
PRUE	Lindsay Duncan
JULIE	Susan Wooldridge
RUSSELL	Steven Pacey
SUKI	Lia Williams
RICHARD	Thomas Wheatley
SONIA	Indira Varma
WAITER	Danny Dyer
WAITRESS 1	Nina Raine
WAITRESS 2	Katherine Tozer

Directed by Harold Pinter
Designed by Eileen Diss

TABLE ONE

WAITER

Who's having the duck?

LAMBERT

The duck's for me.

JULIE

No it isn't.

LAMBERT

No it isn't. Who's it for?

JULIE

Me.

LAMBERT

What am I having? I thought I was having the duck?

JULIE

(*To* WAITER) The duck's for me.

MATT

(*To* WAITER) Chicken for my wife, steak for me.

WAITER

Chicken for the lady.

PRUE

Thank you so much.

WAITER

And who's having the steak?

MATT

Me.

He picks up a wine bottle and pours.

Here we are. Frascati for the ladies. And Valpolicella for me.

LAMBERT

And for me. I mean what about me? What did I order? I haven't the faintest idea. What did I order?

JULIE

Who cares?

LAMBERT

Who cares? I bloody care.

PRUE

Osso Bucco.

LAMBERT

Osso what?

440

PRUE

Bucco.

MATT

It's an old Italian dish.

LAMBERT

Well I knew Osso was Italian but I know bugger all about Bucco.

MATT

I didn't know arsehole was Italian.

LAMBERT

Yes, but on the other hand what's the Italian for arsehole?

PRUE

Julie, Lambert. Happy anniversary.

MATT

Cheers.

They lift their glasses and drink.

TABLE TWO

RUSSELL

They believe in me.

SUKI

Who do?

RUSSELL

They do. What do you mean, who do? They do.

SUKI

Oh, do they?

RUSSELL

Yes, they believe in me. They reckon me. They're
investing in me. In my nous. They believe in me.

SUKI

Listen. I believe you. Honestly. I do. No really,
honestly. I'm sure they believe in you. And they're
right to believe in you. I mean, listen, I want you to be
rich, believe me, I want you to be rich so that you can
buy me houses and panties and I'll know that you
really love me.

They drink.

RUSSELL

Listen, she was just a secretary. That's all. No more.

442

SUKI

Like me.

RUSSELL

What do you mean, like you? She was nothing like you.

SUKI

I was a secretary once.

RUSSELL

She was a scrubber. A scrubber. They're all the same, these secretaries, these scrubbers. They're like politicians. They love power. They've got a bit of power, they use it. They go home, they get on the phone, they tell their girlfriends, they have a good laugh. Listen to me. I'm being honest. You won't find many like me. I fell for it. I've admitted it. She just twisted me round her little finger.

SUKI

That's funny. I thought she twisted you round *your* little finger.

Pause.

RUSSELL

You don't know what these girls are like. These secretaries.

SUKI

Oh I think I do.

RUSSELL

You don't.

SUKI

Oh I do.

RUSSELL

What do you mean, you do?

SUKI

I've been behind a few filing cabinets.

RUSSELL

What?

SUKI

In my time. When I was a plump young secretary.
I know what the back of a filing cabinet looks like.

RUSSELL

Oh do you?

SUKI

Oh yes. Listen. I would invest in you myself if I had
any money. Do you know why? Because I believe in
you.

RUSSELL

What's all this about filing cabinets?

SUKI

Oh that was when I was a plump young secretary.
I would never do all those things now. Never. Out
of the question. You see, the trouble was I was so
excitable, their excitement made me so excited, but
I would never do all those things now I'm a grown-up
woman and not a silly young thing, a silly and dizzy
young girl, such a naughty, saucy, flirty, giggly young
thing, sometimes I could hardly walk from one filing
cabinet to another I was so excited, I was so plump
and wobbly it was terrible, men simply couldn't keep
their hands off me, their demands were outrageous,
but coming back to more important things, they're
right to believe in you, why shouldn't they believe in
you?

TABLE ONE

JULIE

I've always told him. Always. But he doesn't listen.
I tell him all the time. But he doesn't listen.

PRUE

You mean he just doesn't listen?

JULIE

I tell him all the time.

PRUE

(*To* LAMBERT) Why don't you listen to your wife?
She stands by you through thick and thin. You've got
a loyal wife there and never forget it.

LAMBERT

I've got a loyal wife where?

PRUE

Here! At this table.

LAMBERT

I've got one under the table, take my tip.

He looks under the table.

Christ. She's really loyal under the table. Always has
been. You wouldn't believe it.

JULIE

Why don't you go and buy a new car and drive it into
a brick wall?

LAMBERT

She loves me.

MATT

No, she loves new cars.

LAMBERT

With soft leather seats.

MATT

There was a song once.

LAMBERT

How did it go?

MATT

Ain't she neat?
Ain't she neat?
As she's walking up the street.
She's got a lovely bubbly pair of tits
And a soft leather seat.

LAMBERT

That's a really beautiful song.

MATT

I've always admired that song. You know what it is?
It's a traditional folk song.

447

LAMBERT

It's got class.

MATT

It's got tradition and class.

LAMBERT

They don't grow on trees.

MATT

Too bloody right.

LAMBERT

Hey Matt!

MATT

What?

LAMBERT *picks up the bottle of Valpolicella. It is empty.*

LAMBERT

There's something wrong with this bottle.

MATT *turns and calls.*

MATT

Waiter!

TABLE TWO

RUSSELL

All right. Tell me. Do you think I have a nice
character?

SUKI

Yes I think you do. I think you do. I mean I think you
do. Well . . . I mean . . . I think you could have quite
a nice character but the trouble is that when you come
down to it you haven't actually got any character to
begin with – I mean as such, that's the thing.

RUSSELL

As such?

SUKI

Yes, the thing is you haven't really got any character
at all, have you? As such. Au fond. But I wouldn't
worry about it. For example look at me. I don't have
any character either. I'm just a reed. I'm just a reed in
the wind. Aren't I? You know I am. I'm just a reed in
the wind.

RUSSELL

You're a whore.

SUKI

A whore in the wind.

RUSSELL

With the wind blowing up your skirt.

SUKI

That's right. How did you know? How did you know
the sensation? I didn't know that men could possibly
know about that kind of thing. I mean men don't
wear skirts. So I didn't think men could possibly
know what it was like when the wind blows up a
girl's skirt. Because men don't wear skirts.

RUSSELL

You're a prick.

SUKI

Not quite.

RUSSELL

You're a prick.

SUKI

Good gracious. Am I really?

RUSSELL

Yes. That's what you are really.

SUKI

Am I really?

RUSSELL

Yes. That's what you are really.

TABLE ONE

LAMBERT

What's that other song you know? The one you said
was a classic.

MATT

Wash me in the water
Where you washed your dirty daughter.

LAMBERT

That's it. (*To* JULIE) Know that one?

JULIE

It's not in my repertoire, darling.

LAMBERT

This is the best restaurant in town. That's what they
say.

MATT

That's what they say.

LAMBERT

This is a piss-up dinner. Do you know how much
money I made last year?

MATT

I know this is a piss-up dinner.

LAMBERT

It is a piss-up dinner.

PRUE

(*To* JULIE) His mother always hated me. The first time she saw me she hated me. She never gave me one present in the whole of her life. Nothing. She wouldn't give me the drippings off her nose.

JULIE

I know.

PRUE

The drippings off her nose. Honestly.

JULIE

All mothers-in-law are like that. They love their sons. They love their boys. They don't want their sons to be fucked by other girls. Isn't that right?

PRUE

Absolutely. All mothers want their sons to be fucked by themselves.

JULIE

By their mothers.

PRUE

All mothers –

LAMBERT

All mothers want to be fucked by their mothers.

MATT

Or by themselves.

PRUE

No, you've got it the wrong way round.

LAMBERT

How's that?

MATT

All mothers want to be fucked by their sons.

LAMBERT

Now wait a minute –

MATT

My point is –

LAMBERT

No my point is – how old do you have to be?

JULIE

To be what?

LAMBERT

To be fucked by your mother.

MATT

Any age, mate. Any age.

They all drink.

LAMBERT
How did you enjoy your dinner, darling?

JULIE
I wasn't impressed.

LAMBERT
You weren't impressed?

JULIE
No.

LAMBERT
I bring her to the best caff in town – spending a fortune – and she's not impressed.

MATT
Don't forget this is your anniversary. That's why we're here.

LAMBERT
What anniversary?

PRUE
It's your wedding anniversary.

LAMBERT
All I know is this is the most expensive fucking restaurant in town and she's not impressed.

454

RICHARD *comes to the table.*

RICHARD

Good evening.

MATT

Good evening.

PRUE

Good evening.

JULIE

Good evening.

LAMBERT

Good evening, Richard. How you been?

RICHARD

Very very well. Been to a play?

MATT

No. The ballet.

RICHARD

Oh the ballet? What was it?

LAMBERT

That's a fucking good question.

MATT

It's unanswerable.

RICHARD

Good, was it?

LAMBERT

Unbelievable.

JULIE

What ballet?

MATT

None of them could reach the top notes. Could they?

RICHARD

Good dinner?

MATT

Fantastic.

LAMBERT

Top notch. Gold plated.

PRUE

Delicious.

LAMBERT

My wife wasn't impressed.

RICHARD

Oh really?

JULIE

I liked the waiter.

RICHARD

Which one?

JULIE

The one with the fur-lined jockstrap.

LAMBERT

He takes it off for breakfast.

JULIE

Which is more than you do.

RICHARD

Well how nice to see you all.

PRUE

She wasn't impressed with her food. It's true. She said
so. She thought it was dry as dust. She said – what did
you say darling? – she's my sister – she said she could
cook better than that with one hand stuffed between
her legs – she said – no, honestly – she said she could
make a better sauce than the one on that plate if she
pissed into it. Don't think she was joking – she's my
sister, I've known her all my life, all my life, since we
were little innocent girls, all our lives, when we were
babies, when we used to lie in the nursery and hear
mummy beating the shit out of daddy. We saw the
blood on the sheets the next day – when nanny was in
the pantry – my sister and me – and nanny was in the
pantry – and the pantry maid was in the larder and
the parlour maid was in the laundry room washing

the blood out of the sheets. That's how my little sister
and I were brought up and she could make a better
sauce than yours if she pissed into it.

MATT

Well, it's lovely to be here, I'll say that.

LAMBERT

Lovely to be here.

JULIE

Lovely. Lovely.

MATT

Really lovely.

RICHARD

Thank you.

PRUE *stands and goes to* RICHARD.

PRUE

Can I thank you? Can I thank you personally? I'd like
to thank you myself, in my own way.

RICHARD

Well thank you.

PRUE

No no, I'd really like to thank you in a very personal
way.

458

CELEBRATION

JULIE

She'd like to give you her personal thanks.

PRUE

Will you let me kiss you? I'd like to kiss you on the mouth?

JULIE

That's funny. I'd like to kiss him on the mouth too.

She stands and goes to him.

Because I've been maligned, I've been misrepresented. I never said I didn't like your sauce. I love your sauce.

PRUE

We can't both kiss him on the mouth at the same time.

LAMBERT

You could tickle his arse with a feather.

RICHARD

Well I'm so glad. I'm really glad. See you later I hope.

He goes. PRUE *and* JULIE *sit.*

Silence.

MATT

Charming man.

459

LAMBERT

That's why this is the best and most expensive
restaurant in the whole of Europe – because he *insists*
upon proper standards, he *insists* that standards are
maintained with the utmost rigour, you get me? That
standards are maintained up to the highest standards,
up to the very highest fucking standards –

MATT

He doesn't jib.

LAMBERT

Jib? Of course he doesn't jib – it would be more than
his life was worth. He jibs at nothing!

PRUE

I knew him in the old days.

MATT

What do you mean?

PRUE

When he was a chef.

Lambert's mobile phone rings.

LAMBERT

Who the fuck's this?

He switches it on.

Yes? What?

He listens briefly.

I said no calls! It's my fucking wedding anniversary!

He switches it off.

Cunt.

TABLE TWO

SUKI

I'm so proud of you.

RUSSELL

Yes?

SUKI

And I know these people are good people. These
people who believe in you. They're good people.
Aren't they?

RUSSELL

Very good people.

SUKI

And when I meet them, when you introduce me to
them, they'll treat me with respect, won't they? They
won't want to fuck me behind a filing cabinet?

SONIA *comes to the table.*

SONIA

Good evening.

RUSSELL

Good evening.

462

SUKI

Good evening.

SONIA

Everything all right?

RUSSELL

Wonderful.

SONIA

No complaints?

RUSSELL

Absolutely no complaints whatsoever. Absolutely
numero uno all along the line.

SONIA

What a lovely compliment.

RUSSELL

Heartfelt.

SONIA

Been to the theatre?

SUKI

The opera.

SONIA

Oh really, what was it?

SUKI

Well . . . there was a lot going on. A lot of singing.
A great deal, as a matter of fact. They never stopped.
Did they?

RUSSELL

(*To* SONIA) Listen, let me ask you something.

SONIA

You can ask me absolutely anything you like.

RUSSELL

What was your upbringing?

SONIA

That's funny. Everybody asks me that. Everybody
seems to find that an interesting subject. I don't know
why. Isn't it funny? So many people express curiosity
about my upbringing. I've no idea why. What you
really mean of course is – how did I arrive at the
position I hold now – maîtresse d'hôtel – isn't that
right? Isn't that your question? Well, I was born in
Bethnal Green. My mother was a chiropodist. I had
no father.

RUSSELL

Fantastic.

SONIA

Are you going to try our bread-and-butter pudding?

RUSSELL

In spades.

SONIA *smiles and goes.*

RUSSELL

Did I ever tell you about my mother's bread-and-butter pudding?

SUKI

You never have. Please tell me.

RUSSELL

You really want me to tell you? You're not being insincere?

SUKI

Darling. Give me your hand. There. I have your hand. I'm holding your hand. Now please tell me. Please tell me about your mother's bread-and-butter pudding. What was it like?

RUSSELL

It was like drowning in an ocean of richness.

SUKI

How beautiful. You're a poet.

RUSSELL

I wanted to be a poet once. But I got no encouragement from my dad. He thought I was an arsehole.

SUKI

He was jealous of you, that's all. He saw you as a
threat. He thought you wanted to steal his wife.

RUSSELL

His wife?

SUKI

Well, you know what they say.

RUSSELL

What?

SUKI

Oh, you know what they say.

The WAITER *comes to the table and pours wine.*

WAITER

Do you mind if I interject?

RUSSELL

Eh?

WAITER

I say, do you mind if I make an interjection?

SUKI

We'd welcome it.

WAITER

It's just that I heard you talking about T. S. Eliot a
little bit earlier this evening.

SUKI

Oh you heard that, did you?

WAITER

I did. And I thought you might be interested to know
that my grandfather knew T. S. Eliot quite well.

SUKI

Really?

WAITER

I'm not claiming that he was a close friend of his.
But he was a damn sight more than a nodding
acquaintance. He knew them all in fact, Ezra Pound,
W. H. Auden, C. Day Lewis, Louis MacNeice,
Stephen Spender, George Barker, Dylan Thomas and
if you go back a few years he was a bit of a drinking
companion of D. H. Lawrence, Joseph Conrad,
Ford Madox Ford, W. B. Yeats, Aldous Huxley,
Virginia Woolf and Thomas Hardy in his dotage.
My grandfather was carving out a niche for himself
in politics at the time. Some saw him as a future
Chancellor of the Exchequer or at least First Lord
of the Admiralty but he decided instead to command
a battalion in the Spanish Civil War but as things
turned out he spent most of his spare time in the
United States where he was a very close pal of Ernest

Hemingway – they used to play gin rummy together
until the cows came home. But he was also boon
compatriots with William Faulkner, Scott Fitzgerald,
Upton Sinclair, John Dos Passos – you know – that
whole vivid Chicago gang – not to mention John
Steinbeck, Erskine Caldwell, Carson McCullers and
other members of the old Deep South conglomerate.
I mean – what I'm trying to say is – that as a man my
grandfather was just about as all round as you can
get. He was never without his pocket bible and he was
a dab hand at pocket billiards. He stood four square
in the centre of the intellectual and literary life of the
tens, twenties and thirties. He was James Joyce's
godmother.

Silence.

RUSSELL

Have you been working here long?

WAITER

Years.

RUSSELL

You going to stay until it changes hands?

WAITER

Are you suggesting that I'm about to get the boot?

SUKI

They wouldn't do that to a nice lad like you.

468

WAITER

To be brutally honest, I don't think I'd recover if they did a thing like that. This place is like a womb to me. I prefer to stay in my womb. I strongly prefer that to being born.

RUSSELL

I don't blame you. Listen, next time we're talking about T. S. Eliot I'll drop you a card.

WAITER

You would make me a very happy man. Thank you. Thank you. You are incredibly gracious people.

SUKI

How sweet of you.

WAITER

Gracious and graceful.

He goes.

SUKI

What a nice young man.

CELEBRATION

TABLE ONE

LAMBERT

You won't believe this. You're not going to believe
this – and I'm only saying this because I'm among
friends – and I know I'm well liked because I trust my
family and my friends – because I know they like me
fundamentally – you know – deep down they trust
me – deep down they respect me – otherwise I wouldn't
say this. I wouldn't take you all into my confidence if
I thought you all hated my guts – I couldn't be open
and honest with you if I thought you thought I was
a pile of shit. If I thought you would like to see me
hung, drawn and fucking quartered – I could never
be frank and honest with you if that was the truth –
never . . .

Silence.

But as I was about to say, you won't believe this, I fell
in love once and this girl I fell in love with loved me
back. I know she did.

Pause.

JULIE

Wasn't that me, darling?

LAMBERT

Who?

MATT

Her.

LAMBERT

Her? No, not her. A girl. I used to take her for walks
along the river.

JULIE

Lambert fell in love with me on the top of a bus. It
was a short journey. Fulham Broadway to Shepherd's
Bush, but it was enough. He was trembling all over.
I remember. (*To* PRUE) When I got home I came and
sat on your bed, didn't I?

LAMBERT

I used to take this girl for walks along the river. I was
young, I wasn't much more than a nipper.

MATT

That's funny. I never knew anything about that. And
I knew you quite well, didn't I?

LAMBERT

What do you mean you knew me quite well? You
knew nothing about me. You know nothing about me.
Who the fuck are you anyway?

MATT

I'm your big brother.

LAMBERT

I'm talking about love, mate. You know, real fucking
love, walking along the banks of a river holding
hands.

MATT

I saw him the day he was born. You know what he
looked like? An alcoholic. Pissed as a newt. He could
hardly stand.

JULIE

He was trembling like a leaf on top of that bus. I'll
never forget it.

PRUE

I was there when you came home. I remember what
you said. You came into my room. You sat down on
my bed.

MATT

What did she say?

PRUE

I mean we were sisters, weren't we?

MATT

Well, what did she say?

PRUE

I'll never forget what you said. You sat on my bed.
Didn't you? Do you remember?

LAMBERT

This girl was in love with me – I'm trying to tell you.

PRUE

Do you remember what you said?

TABLE TWO

Richard comes to the table.

RICHARD

Good evening.

RUSSELL

Good evening.

SUKI

Good evening.

RICHARD

Everything in order?

RUSSELL

First class.

RICHARD

I'm so glad.

SUKI

Can I say something?

RICHARD

But indeed –

SUKI

Everyone is so happy in your restaurant. I mean women *and* men. You make people so happy.

RICHARD

Well, we do like to feel that it's a happy restaurant.

RUSSELL

It is a happy restaurant. For example, look at me.
Look at me. I'm basically a totally disordered
personality, some people would describe me as a
psychopath. (*To* SUKI) Am I right?

SUKI

Yes.

RUSSELL

But when I'm sitting in this restaurant I suddenly
find I have no psychopathic tendencies at all. I don't
feel like killing everyone in sight, I don't feel like
putting a bomb under everyone's arse. I feel something
quite different, I have a sense of equilibrium, of
harmony, I love my fellow diners. Now this is very
unusual for me. Normally I feel – as I've just said –
absolutely malice and hatred towards everyone within
spitting distance – but here I feel love. How do you
explain it?

SUKI

It's the ambience.

RICHARD

Yes, I think ambience is that intangible thing that
cannot be defined.

RUSSELL

Quite right.

SUKI

It is intangible. You're absolutely right.

RUSSELL

Absolutely.

RICHARD

That is absolutely right. But it does – I would freely admit – exist. It's something you find you are part of. Without knowing exactly what it is.

RUSSELL

Yes. I had an old schoolmaster once who used to say that ambience surrounds you. He never stopped saying that. He lived in a little house in a nice little village but none of us boys were ever invited to tea.

RICHARD

Yes, it's funny you should say that. I was brought up in a little village myself.

SUKI

No? Were you?

RICHARD

Yes, isn't it odd? In a little village in the country.

RUSSELL

What, right in the country?

RICHARD

Oh, absolutely. And my father once took me to our
village pub. I was only that high. Too young to join
him for his pint of course. But I did look in. Black
beams.

RUSSELL

On the roof?

RICHARD

Well, holding the ceiling up in fact. Old men smoking
pipes, no music of course, cheese rolls, gherkins,
happiness. I think this restaurant – which you so
kindly patronise – was inspired by that pub in my
childhood. I do hope you noticed that you have
complimentary gherkins as soon as you take your
seat.

SUKI

That was you! That was your idea!

RICHARD

I believe the concept of this restaurant rests in that
public house of my childhood.

SUKI

I find that incredibly moving.

TABLE ONE

LAMBERT

I'd like to raise my glass.

MATT

What to?

LAMBERT

To my wife. To our anniversary.

JULIE

Oh darling! You remembered!

LAMBERT

I'd like to raise my glass. I ask you to raise your
glasses to my wife.

JULIE

I'm so touched by this, honestly. I mean I have to
say –

LAMBERT

Raise your fucking glass and shut up!

JULIE

But darling, that's naked aggression. He doesn't
normally go in for naked aggression. He usually
disguises it under honeyed words. What is it sweetie?
He's got a cold in the nose, that's what it is.

478

LAMBERT

I want us to drink to our anniversary. We've been married for more bloody years than I can remember and it don't seem a day too long.

PRUE

Cheers.

MATT

Cheers.

JULIE

It's funny our children aren't here. When they were young we spent so much time with them, the little things, looking after them.

PRUE

I know.

JULIE

Playing with them.

PRUE

Feeding them.

JULIE

Being their mothers.

PRUE

They always loved me much more than they loved him.

JULIE

Me too. They loved me to distraction. I was their
mother.

PRUE

Yes, I was too. I was my children's mother.

MATT

They have no memory.

LAMBERT

Who?

MATT

Children. They have no memory. They remember
nothing. They don't remember who their father was
or who their mother was. It's all a hole in the wall for
them. They don't remember their own life.

SONIA *comes to the table.*

SONIA

Everything all right?

JULIE

Perfect.

SONIA

Were you at the opera this evening?

JULIE

No.

PRUE

No.

SONIA

Theatre?

PRUE

No.

JULIE

No.

MATT

This is a celebration.

SONIA

Oh my goodness! A birthday?

MATT

Anniversary.

PRUE

My sister and her husband. Anniversary of their
marriage. I was her leading bridesmaid.

MATT

I was his best man.

LAMBERT

I was just about to fuck her at the altar when
somebody stopped me.

SONIA

Really?

MATT

I stopped him. His zip went down and I kicked him up the arse. It would have been a scandal. The world's press was on the doorstep.

JULIE

He was always impetuous.

SONIA

We get so many different kinds of people in here, people from all walks of life.

PRUE

Do you really?

SONIA

Oh yes. People from all walks of life. People from different countries. I've often said, 'You don't have to speak English to enjoy good food.' I've often said that. Or even understand English. It's like sex isn't it? You don't have to be English to enjoy sex. You don't have to speak English to enjoy sex. Lots of people enjoy sex without being English. I've known one or two Belgian people for example who love sex and they don't speak a word of English. The same applies to Hungarians.

LAMBERT

Yes. I met a chap who was born in Venezuela once
and he didn't speak a fucking word of English.

MATT

Did he enjoy sex?

LAMBERT

Sex?

SONIA

Yes, it's funny you should say that. I met a man from
Morocco once and he was very interested in sex.

JULIE

What happened to him?

SONIA

Now you've upset me. I think I'm going to cry.

PRUE

Oh, poor dear. Did he let you down?

SONIA

He's dead. He died in another woman's arms. He was
on the job. Can you see how tragic my life has been?

Pause.

MATT

Well, I can. I don't know about the others.

JULIE

I can too.

PRUE

So can I.

SONIA

Have a happy night.

She goes.

LAMBERT

Lovely woman.

The WAITER *comes to the table and pours wine into their glasses.*

WAITER

Do you mind if I interject?

MATT

What?

WAITER

Do you mind if I make an interjection?

MATT

Help yourself.

WAITER

It's just that a little bit earlier I heard you saying

something about the Hollywood studio system in the thirties.

PRUE

Oh you heard that?

WAITER

Yes. And I thought you might be interested to know that my grandfather was very familiar with a lot of the old Hollywood film stars back in those days. He used to knock about with Clark Gable and Elisha Cook Jr and he was one of the very few native-born Englishmen to have had it off with Hedy Lamarr.

JULIE

No?

LAMBERT

What was she like in the sack?

WAITER

He said she was really tasty.

JULIE

I'll bet she was.

WAITER

Of course there was a very well-established Irish Mafia in Hollywood in those days. And there was a very close connection between some of the famous Irish film stars and some of the famous Irish gangsters

in Chicago. Al Capone and Victor Mature for example.
They were both Irish. Then there was John Dillinger
the celebrated gangster and Gary Cooper the celebrated
film star. They were Jewish.

Silence.

JULIE

It makes you think, doesn't it?

PRUE

It does make you think.

LAMBERT

You see that girl at that table? I know her. I fucked
her when she was eighteen.

JULIE

What, by the banks of the river?

LAMBERT *waves at* SUKI. SUKI *waves back. She
whispers to* RUSSELL, *gets up and goes to Lambert's
table followed by* RUSSELL.

SUKI

Lambert! It's you!

LAMBERT

Suki! You remember me!

SUKI

Do you remember me?

LAMBERT

Do I remember you? *Do* I remember you!

SUKI

This is my husband Russell.

LAMBERT

Hello Russell.

RUSSELL

Hello Lambert.

LAMBERT

This is my wife Julie.

JULIE

Hello Suki.

SUKI

Hello Julie.

RUSSELL

Hello Julie.

JULIE

Hello Russell.

LAMBERT

And this is my brother Matt.

MATT

Hello Suki, hello Russell.

SUKI

Hello Matt.

RUSSELL

Hello Matt.

LAMBERT

And this is his wife Prue. She's Julie's sister.

SUKI

She's not!

PRUE

Yes, we're sisters and they're brothers.

SUKI

They're not!

RUSSELL

Hello Prue.

PRUE

Hello Russell.

SUKI

Hello Prue.

PRUE

Hello Suki.

LAMBERT

Sit down. Squeeze in. Have a drink.

They sit.

What'll you have?

RUSSELL

A drop of that red wine would work wonders.

LAMBERT

Suki?

RUSSELL

She'll have the same.

SUKI

(*To* LAMBERT) Are you still obsessed with gardening?

LAMBERT

Me?

SUKI

(*To* JULIE) When I knew him he was absolutely obsessed with gardening.

LAMBERT

Yes, well, I would say I'm still moderately obsessed with gardening.

JULIE

He likes grass.

LAMBERT

It's true. I love grass.

JULIE

Green grass.

SUKI

You used to love flowers, didn't you? Do you still love
flowers?

JULIE

He adores flowers. The other day I saw him emptying
a piss pot into a bowl of lilies.

RUSSELL

My dad was a gardener.

MATT

Not your grandad?

RUSSELL

No, my dad.

SUKI

That's right, he was. He was always walking about
with a lawn mower.

LAMBERT

What, even in the Old Kent Road?

RUSSELL

He was a man of the soil.

MATT

How about your grandad?

RUSSELL

I never had one.

JULIE

Funny that when you knew my husband you thought he was obsessed with gardening. I always thought he was obsessed with girls' bums.

SUKI

Really?

PRUE

Oh yes, he was always a keen wobbler.

MATT

What do you mean? How do you know?

PRUE

Oh don't get excited. It's all in the past.

MATT

What is?

SUKI

I sometimes feel that the past is never past.

RUSSELL

What do you mean?

JULIE

You mean that yesterday is today?

SUKI

That's right. You feel the same, do you?

JULIE

I do.

MATT

Bollocks.

JULIE

I wouldn't like to live again though, would you? Once is more than enough.

LAMBERT

I'd like to live again. In fact I'm going to make it my job to live again. I'm going to come back as a better person, a more civilised person, a gentler person, a nicer person.

JULIE

Impossible.

Pause.

PRUE

I wonder where these two met? I mean Lambert and
Suki.

RUSSELL

Behind a filing cabinet.

Silence.

JULIE

What is a filing cabinet?

RUSSELL

It's a thing you get behind.

Pause.

LAMBERT

No, not me mate. You've got the wrong bloke. I agree
with my wife. I don't even know what a filing cabinet
looks like. I wouldn't know a filing cabinet if I met
one coming round the corner.

Pause.

JULIE

So what's your job now then, Suki?

SUKI

Oh, I'm a schoolteacher now. I teach infants.

PRUE

What, little boys and little girls?

SUKI

What about you?

PRUE

Oh, Julie and me – we run charities. We do charities.

RUSSELL

Must be pretty demanding work.

JULIE

Yes, we're at it day and night, aren't we?

PRUE

Well, there are so many worthy causes.

MATT

(*To* RUSSELL) You're a banker? Right?

RUSSELL

That's right.

MATT

(*To* LAMBERT) He's a banker.

LAMBERT

With a big future before him.

MATT

Well that's what he reckons.

LAMBERT

I want to ask you a question. How did you know he was a banker?

MATT

Well it's the way he holds himself, isn't it?

LAMBERT

Oh, yes.

SUKI

What about you two?

LAMBERT

Us two?

SUKI

Yes.

LAMBERT

Well, we're consultants. Matt and me. Strategy
consultants.

MATT

Strategy consultants.

LAMBERT

It means we don't carry guns.

MATT *and* LAMBERT *laugh.*

We don't have to!

MATT

We're peaceful strategy consultants.

LAMBERT

Worldwide. Keeping the peace.

RUSSELL

Wonderful.

LAMBERT

Eh?

RUSSELL

Really impressive. We need a few more of you about.

Pause.

We need more people like you. Taking responsibility.
Taking charge. Keeping the peace. Enforcing the
peace. Enforcing peace. We need more like you.
I think I'll have a word with my bank. I'm moving
any minute to a more substantial bank. I'll have
a word with them. I'll suggest lunch. In the City.
I know the ideal restaurant. All the waitresses have
big tits.

SUKI

Aren't you pushing the tits bit a bit far?

RUSSELL

Me? I thought you did that.

Pause.

LAMBERT

Be careful. You're talking to your wife.

MATT

Have some respect, mate.

LAMBERT

Have respect. That's all we ask.

MATT

It's not much to ask.

LAMBERT

But it's crucial.

Pause.

RUSSELL
So how is the strategic consultancy business these days?

LAMBERT
Very good, old boy. Very good.

MATT
Very good. We're at the receiving end of some of the best tea in China.

RICHARD *and* SONIA *come to the table with a magnum of champagne, the* WAITER *with a tray of glasses. Everyone gasps.*

RICHARD
To celebrate a treasured wedding anniversary.

MATT *looks at the label on the bottle.*

MATT
That's the best of the best.

The bottle opens. RICHARD *pours.*

LAMBERT
And may the best man win!

JULIE
The woman always wins.

PRUE

Always.

SUKI

That's really good news.

PRUE

The woman always wins.

RICHARD *and* SONIA *raise their glasses.*

RICHARD

To the happy couple. God bless. God bless you all.

EVERYONE

Cheers. Cheers . . .

MATT

What a wonderful restaurant this is.

SONIA

Well, we do care. I will say that. We care. That's the point. Don't we?

RICHARD

Yes. We do care. We care about the welfare of our clientele. I will say that.

LAMBERT *stands and goes to them.*

LAMBERT

What you say means so much to me. Let me give you a cuddle.

He cuddles RICHARD.

And let me give you a cuddle.

He cuddles SONIA.

This is so totally rare, you see. None of this normally happens. People normally – you know – people normally are so distant from each other. That's what I've found. Take a given bloke – this given bloke doesn't know that another given bloke exists. It goes down through history, doesn't it?

MATT

It does.

LAMBERT

One bloke doesn't know that another bloke exists. Generally speaking. I've often noticed.

SONIA

(*To* JULIE *and* PRUE) I'm so touched that you're sisters. I had a sister. But she married a foreigner and I haven't seen her since.

PRUE

Some foreigners are all right.

SONIA

Oh I think foreigners are charming. Most people
in this restaurant tonight are foreigners. My sister's
husband had a lot of charm but he also had an
enormous moustache. I had to kiss him at the
wedding. I can't describe how awful it was. I've
got such soft skin, you see.

WAITER

Do you mind if I interject?

RICHARD

I'm sorry?

WAITER

Do you mind if I make an interjection?

RICHARD

What on earth do you mean?

WAITER

Well, it's just that I heard all these people talking
about the Austro-Hungarian Empire a little while
ago and I wondered if they'd ever heard about my
grandfather. He was an incredibly close friend of the
Archduke himself and he once had a cup of tea with
Benito Mussolini. They all played poker together,
Winston Churchill included. The funny thing about
my grandfather was that the palms of his hands
always seemed to be burning. But his eyes were
elsewhere. He had a really strange life. He was in

love, he told me, once, with the woman who turned out to be my grandmother, but he lost her somewhere. She disappeared, I think, in a sandstorm. In the desert. My grandfather was everything men aspired to be in those days. He was tall, dark and handsome. He was full of good will. He'd even give a cripple with no legs crawling on his belly through the slush and mud of a country lane a helping hand. He'd lift him up, he'd show him his way, he'd point him in the right direction. He was like Jesus Christ in that respect. And he was gregarious. He loved the society of his fellows, W. B. Yeats, T. S. Eliot, Igor Stravinsky, Picasso, Ezra Pound, Bertholt Brecht, Don Bradman, the Beverley Sisters, the Inkspots, Franz Kafka and the Three Stooges. He knew these people where they were isolated, where they were alone, where they fought against savage and pitiless odds, where they suffered vast wounds to their bodies, their bellies, their legs, their trunks, their eyes, their throats, their breasts, their balls –

LAMBERT

(*Standing*) Well, Richard – what a great dinner!

RICHARD

I'm so glad.

LAMBERT *opens his wallet and unpeels fifty-pound notes. He gives two to* RICHARD.

LAMBERT

This is for you.

RICHARD

No, no really –

LAMBERT

No no, this is for you. (*To* SONIA) And this is for you.

SONIA

Oh, no please –

LAMBERT *dangles the notes in front of her cleavage.*

LAMBERT

Shall I put them down here?

SONIA *giggles.*

No I'll tell you what – you wearing suspenders?

SONIA *giggles.*

Stick them in your suspenders. (*To* WAITER) Here you are son. Mind how you go.

Puts a note into his pocket.

Great dinner. Great restaurant. Best in the country.

MATT

Best in the world I'd say.

LAMBERT
Exactly. (*To* RICHARD) I'm taking their bill.

RUSSELL
No, no you can't –

LAMBERT
It's my wedding anniversary! Right? (*To* RICHARD)
Send me their bill.

JULIE
And his.

LAMBERT
Send me both bills. Anyway . . .

He embraces SUKI.

It's for old time's sake as well, right?

SUKI
Right.

RICHARD
See you again soon?

MATT
Absolutely.

SONIA
See you again soon.

PRUE

Absolutely.

SONIA

Next celebration?

JULIE

Absolutely.

LAMBERT

Plenty of celebrations to come. Rest assured.

MATT

Plenty to celebrate.

LAMBERT

Dead right.

MATT *slaps his thighs.*

MATT

Like – who's in front? Who's in front?

LAMBERT *joins in the song, slapping his thighs in time with* MATT.

LAMBERT *and* MATT

Who's in front?
Who's in front?

LAMBERT

Get out the bloody way
You silly old cunt!

LAMBERT *and* MATT *laugh.*

SUKI *and* RUSSELL *go to their table to collect*
handbag and jacket, etc.

SUKI

How sweet of him to take the bill, wasn't it?

RUSSELL

He must have been very fond of you.

SUKI

Oh he wasn't all that fond of me really. He just liked
my . . . oh . . . you know . . .

RUSSELL

Your what?

SUKI

Oh . . . my . . . you know . . .

LAMBERT

Fabulous evening.

JULIE

Fabulous.

RICHARD

See you soon then.

SONIA

See you soon.

MATT

I'll be here for breakfast tomorrow morning.

SONIA

Excellent!

PRUE

See you soon.

SONIA

See you soon.

JULIE

Lovely to see you.

SONIA

See you soon I hope.

RUSSELL

See you soon.

SUKI

See you soon.

They drift off.

JULIE (*off*)

So lovely to meet you.

SUKI (*off*)

Lovely to meet you.

Silence.

The WAITER *stands alone.*

WAITER

When I was a boy my grandfather used to take me to the edge of the cliffs and we'd look out to sea. He bought me a telescope. I don't think they have telescopes any more. I used to look through this telescope and sometimes I'd see a boat. The boat would grow bigger through the telescopic lens. Sometimes I'd see people on the boat. A man, sometimes, and a woman, or sometimes two men. The sea glistened.

My grandfather introduced me to the mystery of life and I'm still in the middle of it. I can't find the door to get out. My grandfather got out of it. He got right out of it. He left it behind him and he didn't look back.

He got that absolutely right.

And I'd like to make one further interjection.

He stands still.

Slow fade.